Built to Last
Defeat the early failure syndrome

William F. Johnson

DEDICATION

This book is dedicated to the thousands of people who have been hurt financially and emotionally by the failure and closing of businesses and other organizations to which they had become a part..

GET A FREE BOOK @
http://aslanpress.com

ACKNOWLEDGMENTS
First I want to acknowledge my wife, Rita for her love and support throughout our marriage and especially for the last year spent writing this book. We would like to thank Ron and Rebecca Bounds, and Beth Wynn for their encouragement, review, and comments which added to the book's direction and value.

Table of Contents

Other Books by William F Johnson

- Leading Your Ministry to Financial Health
  http://www.aslanpress.com/financial-leadership.html

- Motivation: Your Guide to Fitting In
  http://www.aslanpress.com/motivation.html

- Destiny: Who Am I? Why Am I Here, What Do I Do Now?
  http://www.aslanpress.com/destiny.html

- Physician, Heal Thyself: The Oxygen Mask Principle
  http://www.aslanpress.com/physician-heal-thyself.html

- Pray Like Jesus
  http://aslanpress.com/pray-like-jesus.html

Building to Last

Introduction

Within five years of a start-up, half of the companies - begun with vision, excitement and hope - will no longer exist. Employees, customers, and other associates are left in limbo. Why and how can this be avoided?

The answer could lie in how we characterize the organizations. We get a clue from the word itself. Organizations are living organisms – they consist of real live people. Companies and organizations therefore have a natural life cycle. It begins with the excitement and enthusiasm of the day they open, on to a point of maximum efficiency, then decline and then to closing the doors.

Over the past decades we have seen the results of failed organizations and it is not pretty. The impact on the lives of the people close to them has been devastating. What is doubly tragic is that most of these failures could have been avoided if their leaders had anticipated their future and took steps to avoid the deadly causes.

This book has been written in the hope that older organizations will be transformed and renewed while new start-ups are built to last.

Earlier, I shied away from taking over existing organizations. My preferred position was to start a unit from scratch. I had been a part of organizations in decline, and it was not pretty – watching senior management ignore the situation as they drove the organization – with its employees and customers - over the proverbial cliff. Starting from scratch, would enable me to enjoy the new birth, lead to a point of high efficiency, and then get out before things got rough.

That all changed when starting a new organization with people that had been hurt by an earlier failed start-up. At that point, I determined to learn how to transform a failing enterprise to avoid hurting people.

Building to Last

It doesn't matter if a manufacturing plant closes its doors permanently, or moves to a new less expensive region. The pain of the community's loss is huge. There are many reasons why organizations fail, - often there is not a good solution - but many can be renewed and returned to their previous glory and effectiveness, if someone has the desire to restore what has been lost.

This book provides insight into organizational dynamics in the hopes that a new understanding will lead to practical ideas and concepts that will aid in the process of renewal. We pray that plateaued and declining organizations will rediscover the things that gave the founders so much enthusiasm and hope for the future.

Take an objective look. Is your business or organization at a plateau or in decline? It is not too late for a transformation but it will probably not be easy.

William F Johnson

Chapter 1 - The Birth

It starts with a Vision

At the birth of a baby, the family gathers around. The awesome wonder is exciting. A new life has begun with its future wide open. What will this person accomplish? What will be its destiny? This is a time of anticipation, and big dreams of the future. There is a potential for greatness. But then the parents feel the burden of responsibility. They must provide the child with nurture and resources in order for it to reach its full potential. Many parents fill the child's life with too many organized activities - sports, dancing classes, and church groups. The founder of a new company can make the same mistake. In his or her desire t become instantly profitable, they try to do too many things all at once.

If you do not have a vision of what you want your company to become, wait until you have one.

A great corporate vision requires a great imagination. Unfortunately, the past twenty years of formal business education has deemphasized imagination in favor of rational, logical decision making. Growing up without television, I would sit on the floor listening to the Lone Ranger, Jack Benny, and other programs of that era. As I shut my eyes I could envision the great white stallion, Silver, and the Lone Ranger's trusted Indian friend Tonto. When these programs came to television something was lost. No television set could equal the imagination pictured in a listener's mind.

The state of Mississippi is often listed near the bottom in education and affluence, but it stands out above all other states in the number of creatives per capita. Authors, poets, artists and actors abound. Was there something in the water? As a foreigner, (read Yankee) living and working in that state for many years, I have come to an explanation. Because of the slower lifestyle, people have time to think. When people have time to think, they have time to have a dream, a vision and be creative.

Building to Last

When starting a company from scratch all you have s the vision. There are few (or no) customers. There is a lot of activity, reaching out, meeting people, and establishing products or services. This leaves time for dreaming, envisioning, thinking and soul searching.

You start with the vision of the future, a significant purpose that will motivate your team to spend their lives for that purpose. Concerns and difficulties are subjugated by the sheer power of the vision. The rewards will be greater than the risks. Your family, employees, associates are able to foresee the significance of what they are trying to accomplish.

When tests and trials arise, the vision becomes dimmer in light of immediate problems. The exciting adventure of achieving the vision dims, even in the best of situations. Somewhere along the way, the organization itself changes. Instead of being the instrument for fulfilling the vision, it now has become a consumer of valuable resources. Like an overindulged, spoiled child, the organization itself demands everyone's attention. The vision is subjugated to the demands of maintaining the organization. Resources intended to serve the greater purpose are now consumed maintaining the organization.

Organizations grow into bureaucracies and become more and more demanding consuming more time and resources just to maintain their existence. The leaders, employees, or members become so consumed with keeping the organization fed that they forget the original purpose. Imagine the "Borg Collective,"[1] from the Star Trek television series. The Borg was an alien race that was a collection of species that have

---

[1]   The Borg is a fictional alien race that appears as recurring antagonists in the Star Trek franchise. Aside from being the main threat in First Contact , the Borg play major roles in The Next Generation and Voyager television series, primarily as an invasion threat to the United Federation of Planets , and serve as the way home to the Alpha Quadrant for isolated Federation starship Voyager .

been turned into cybernetic organisms functioning as drones in a hive mind called the Collective, or the hive. The fictional Borg, whose ultimate goal is "achieving perfection," resembles a large organization trying to achieve ultimate institutionalization.

The organization has become institutionalized. It acts like Audrey Jr., the crossbreed of a Butterwort and a Venus Fly Trap in the movie Little Shop of Horrors.[2] As the plant keeps growing, it became more demanding, and commands its owner, "Feed me Seymour!"

Any organization, large or small, can fall into this trap and lose sight of the original significant purpose for which it was created. Governments, corporations, labor unions, service organizations, and religious entities are all vulnerable to losing the dream. The obvious examples of this bureaucratic process are government agencies. But, we see it in the banking industry where a bank becomes "too large to fail." Some corporations grow out of control through merger and acquisition as they attempt to control a business segment. Labor unions, which came into life to protect the workers, have become institutions and have lost sight of their original purpose. Many now exploit workers in the same way the industrial barons once did. Education systems have become large bureaucracies which must be maintained while the education level of students continues to fall. In the old one room country school, the majority of expenditures for education were spent in the classroom. Now the majority of funds are spent on maintaining a bureaucracy. The hierarchy of some charitable organizations

---

[2] **Little Shop of Horrors** is a 1986 American, rock musical, horror, comedy film directed by Frank Oz . It is a film adaptation of the off-Broadway musical comedy of the same name by composer Alan Menken and writer Howard Ashman about a nerdy florist shop worker who raises a vicious, raunchy plant that feeds on human blood.

has grown to the point where only a small fraction (as little as five percent in some well-known cases) of their income is actually spent helping people. The majority of donations feed the organizational beast. Our religious institutions are not immune to this structural obesity. Many local churches spend the majority of their energy and budgets on maintaining facilities and infrastructure. As a result little is left to feed the poor and outreach to the needs of the community they were created to serve.

While this condition is pandemic throughout the world, there are solutions that can bring renewal to these organizations. Renewal infers that there was a significant vision must be rediscovered and realized. Renewal does not refer to the achievement of the dream but to the restoration of the dream that motivated the people to continue to believe in the dream.

What has been lost can still be found, but it requires drastic action. The alternative is to continue on the path of the organization's budgets to grow larger while providing less and less significant work.

This book is based upon real life situations and describes methods for renewing industrial, commercial and religious organizations. The same methods could be used to renew governments, but the political issues are beyond the scope of this project.

What Do We Do Here?

"What do we do here?" The neatly dressed, red haired administrative assistant asked smiling self-consciously. That question had been bugging her since she had been hired a month earlier and was the only employee in the office. Her question was the same thing that the new manager had been asking himself for the past three days while driving across country. He came from a comfortable home and career on the Mississippi Gulf Coast to work for an entirely unknown

4

Washington DC company. He was to manage their new office in San Diego, California. The two thousand mile car trip gave him lots of time to think and have second thoughts about his future, and his concern for his family's ability to adapt to the new life in a new part of the country. He located his new office suite in a strip mall off Mission Gorge Boulevard and sat in the car for several minutes before building up the courage to enter this new life. Always an optimist, he was excited buy realized the personal risks involved. The company he was to work for had been in business for less than three months. It had been started by an ex-marine who lived in a Virginia suburb of Washington D.C. three thousand miles away. The manager's role - as explained by the company founder - was to run the Western Operations, but he was unsure of what those operations consisted. As he looked around the office, that realization hit home. His domain consisted of a receptionist, two desks, and a telephone. But what were they doing here?

As he hesitated to respond to his new assistant's question, she frowned and repeated with urgency of her concern, "No, really, what do we do?"

She was very professional in appearance and demeanor, tall, wearing a tailored suit and her hair well-coiffed, "I was beginning to worry how legitimate we were. All I do is answer the phone and pass on messages. I was beginning to question the legitimacy of this organization."

The new manager built up all of the courage and confidence that he could muster and responded, "I'm not sure what we do here. But we are going to find out together and be successful."

With that answer a new organization was born.

New organizations are normally born out of a passion to change the status quo - to develop a new product, introduce a new service, or fulfill a personal vision of a future outcome. This is the way new churches are started, new businesses

5

formed, and new governments are created. There is something that calls certain people do something that has never been done before. They are the ones who explore new worlds - below the seas, in outer space, and places here that civilization has missed. They are called explorers, missionaries, or entrepreneurs. They have the passion, courage, and tenacity overcome their fears and face the future with abandon. Abraham was called by God to leave his hometown of Ur of the Chaldees and leave his family and go to a land he had never seen.

> ***Genesis 12:1-3 (NKJV)*** *Now the Lord had said to Abram: "Get out of your country, From your family And from your father's house, To a land that I will show you. 2 I will make you a great nation; I will bless you And make your name great; And you shall be a blessing. 3 I will bless those who bless you, And I will curse him who curses you; And in you all the families of the earth shall be blessed."*

Abraham believed God and moved.

In the heart of the new General Manager in San Diego, a vision had been percolating for years - building a world-wide company from scratch that would be recognized for providing excellence in products, service, and expertise. It would be accomplished by identifying customer needs, developing innovative products to meet those needs, and providing the service their customers required.

In San Diego, the original customers were the US Naval activities in the western United States. There was a great need for expertise in very specific areas, and new requirements were discovered daily. The company grew by listening to potential customers and figuring out how this organization could provide solutions.

The organization grew rapidly and structure was added in support of the activities. In ten years it was operating at its highest efficiency and had become an international company with offices around the Pacific Rim. Business was being conducted in India, China, Canada, Japan, the Philippines, South Korea, as well as the United States. The contracts with their original customers had grown over one hundred times the initial contract. Other US government agencies and military services were added to the customer list.

The original vision had been achieved and like explorers, entrepreneurs will always seek mountains to climb and places to explore.

Life Cycle

Somewhere between the tenth and fifteenth year that San Diego organization, and its affiliates, lost sight of the original vision. The founding leaders had moved on to other things and a new management had taken over. The company became institutionalized. It was still effective, but not growing as the focus changed from excellence in customer service to maintaining the organization. In its earlier existence the company was able to win contracts based upon technical skill and a reputation for excellence, it now had to rely on being the lowest bidder.

The company had lost its direction. Customer loyalty had ceased as products and services were reduced in both quantity and quality. Employee morale dropped, overhead increased, and profit margins sunk.

By its twentieth birthday, the organization ceased to exist. It wasn't sudden, it just began to fade away and employees scattered to other places. The organization that had begun with so much energy and hope had been merged, sold and resold until it lost its focus, identity and purpose.

The above true story is not atypical. The statistics of failure rates for start-up companies, new organizations and churches are estimated by both the United States Census Bureau and the Bureau of Labor Statistics.

The graph below plots the percent of start-up companies which are still operating after a certain number of years. This particular graph was prepared in 2010. It shows that after five years, only fifty percent of the start-ups continue in business. After ten years there will be thirty-four percent which are still operating, and only twenty five percent will be in existence after sixteen years.

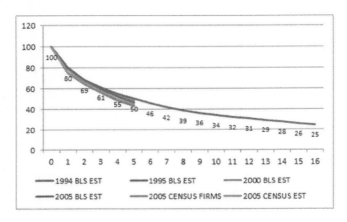

Many factors impact a company's longevity and will be addressed throughout this book.

Creating a new church, business or other organization from scratch is an exciting, and sometimes frightening, experience. Many "would be" entrepreneurs or church planters desire to start their organizations for the wrong reasons. Some may have a great desire to be in control; others are in it to make a lot of quick money, and some desire the recognition and accolades of being a Chief Executive Officer. Starting their own organization may be the only way some can achieve their desires.

Successful entrepreneurs are driven by a passion to create. Their creation may be a product to make life easier, a form of art, or a functional organization. Bill Gates, founder of Microsoft, had a passion for computers. He learned to write software at an early age, and then started his own company with a vision to develop operating systems which could work across all computers. His opportunity came when the government forced IBM to divest itself of their software development business. Gates stepped in and provided the Digital Operating System (DOS) which became the heart of every early personal computer (PC).

Birthing a new organization is not clean and easy. Human babies are not clean and easy. A parent must provide continual care; feeding, bathing, burping, teaching, and cleaning up messes. It is the same with startup companies and church plants, they require constant care, financing, training, and cleaning up messes. In order to survive the first five years the founder must have a strong motivation to continue to fight through all of the unforeseen problems that occur in a startup. It is not as easy as drawing up a business plan, an organization chart, and putting people in the right slots.

The Merriam Webster's on-line dictionary defines an organization as:

"(1.) The act or process of organizing or of being organized, the condition or manner of being organized; (2.) An association, society an administrative, and functional structure (as a business or a political party); also: the personnel of such a structure.

Wikipedia further explains:

"An organization .... is an entity, such as an institution or an association that has a collective goal and is linked to an external environment. The word is derived from the Greek word organon, which is the root of 'organ.'"

It is significant to remember that an organization has a collective goal, is linked to its environment, and is organic in nature. Contrary to traditional thought, an new organization is not a machine to be plugged into a power source, turned on, and watched as it performs its function. It is a living and breathing entity that has a culture, needs to be motivated, and has its own specific personality.

An organization does not exist in isolation; it must interact with its environment. It is not a closed system which acts only within itself. A closed system operates with disregard for its environment. Open systems respond to external forces and adjust to this change.

> *An open system has the capacity to respond to change and disorder by reorganizing itself at a higher level of organization. Disorder becomes a critical player, an ally that can provoke a system to self-organize into new forms of being. As we leave behind the machine model of life and look more deeply into the dynamics of living systems, we begin to glimpse an entirely new way of understanding fluctuations, disorder, and change.*[3]

Organizational theory has evolved over many years and will continue to evolve as our culture and technology evolve.

If an organization were a well-oiled machine it would never change. It would keep working as long as its parts did not wear out and if it did not lose its power source. But organizations are made up of imperfect people who have a limitations and capabilities. Their working life varies with the individual. Empirically, we have observed that organizations go through a process of initial startup, improving, and growing, until they reach their peak performance. Then most tend to decline and finally cease to exist or become ineffective.

---

[3]   Wheatley, Margaret J. (2006-09-01). Leadership and the New Science: Discovering Order in a Chaotic World (Kindle Locations 415-418). Berrett-Koehler Publishers. Kindle Edition.

This is true of business organizations, churches, denominations, government agencies and nations.

On May 19th 1845, Sir John Franklin, with 138 officers and men, sailed from England in search of the Northwest Passage to the Orient. The planned route would take them over the top of North America. Everyone on this voyage was excited about being the first to succeed where others had failed. It was a wonderful send off as they left London. The Royal Navy Band played as Franklin's vessels the "Erebus" and "Terror" sailed along the Thames River to the open sea with thousands of people lining up along the river, cheering and waving British flags. The brave explorers were full of excitement and anticipation. None realized the cost they would pay. They were last seen by the crew of two whaling ships, in Baffin Bay at the end of July. Their dismal failure and the subsequent search for survivors attracted publicity that resulted in a change in Arctic exploration. The Franklin expedition had been more adapted to the conditions in Royal Navy's Officer's club than to arctic conditions. Each ship had an auxiliary steam engine, with only a 12 day supply of coal, for the projected 2-3 year voyage. In place of additional coal, each ship made room for a 1,200 volume library, a hand organ playing fifty tunes, china place settings for the officer's mess, cut glass goblets, sterling silver flat ware, and fine Linens. They had no Arctic clothing, only their naval uniforms. For 20 years search parties recovered skeletons from all over the Arctic Circle. Franklin himself refused to leave the ship and froze to death as the ship was frozen in the ice. Others tried to walk out - but were so overburdened with books, heavy silver, and the china place settings - that they did not get very far. In 1850, near the mouth of Great Fish River, Inuit hunters discovered the bodies of thirty men and a number of graves. As a result of that expedition's publicity and search for survivors, maps were created and Arctic conditions became known to future expeditions who were better prepared.

New organizations often begin their lives like the Franklin expedition - with a dream of success and fame - but without knowledge of the risks involved. Businesses fail due to inadequate financing, lack of planning, and poor preparation. Some are like the Franklyn expedition, they have not done their research, nor have they the experience required for the venture.

The United States Bureau of Labor Statistics reports that less than fifty percent of business start-ups will survive beyond five years. Even when an organization makes it through the initial five years, after seventeen years only one fourth of businesses are still alive.[4] If we are realistic, we must accept that organizations have a specific life-cycle. There are ways to interrupt the inevitable disintegration for a time, but ultimately the cycle continues.

Observing the history of civilization; countries rise up to super power status, begin to decline, and then most cease to exist or are taken over by a new rising state. As Egypt declined in power in the eighth century BCE, the Assyrians, under Tiglath-Pileser III, became the power in the Middle East. Assyria then went into decline as subsequent kings were weak. Assyria was conquered by Babylon which later rose to great power under King Nebuchadnezzar. After his death Babylon declined and was conquered by the Medo-Persian Empire without even a fight. Then the Greeks rose to power when Alexander, The Great, conquered the Medo-Persians and all of the Middle East. Greece declined in power after Alexander's death and the Roman Empire rose up until it too lost its way. Since then we have seen nations rise to power and then fall into decline. Most organizations follow this same path with a limited life.

An analysis of an organization is useful in identifying where it is positioned in its life cycle. The life cycle position of an organization reveals whether the business is growing,

---

[4] http://www.bls.gov/bdm/entrepreneurship/bdm_chart3.htm

stagnant, or declining. This understanding will aid in determining what changes are required.

For simplicity we have chosen to divide the life cycle of an organization into five phases; Initial Structuring, Formal Organization, Maximum Efficiency, Institutionalization, and Disintegration.

These are not the only phases one could identify but they illustrate the point we are making that organizations are fluid and move from phase to phase. There is not a specific time frame for moving through the phases and initiating change could reverse the movement towards its ultimate disintegration.

Initial Structuring

At the starting point of a new organization there is a sense of destiny among the leaders and their initial team of followers.

There is an interesting U-Tube video from the Sasquatch Rock Festival in Washington State. In the hills above the Columbia River there is a large crowd listening to the music. Then one person arises and begins a wild dance. Most people ignore him until another person starts to dance. After this "first follower," others join in the dance until most of the people on the hill side are dancing. But they did not join in until the first follower began to dance.[5]

In the beginning of an organization, church, or business, the Utopian future is just over the horizon. Some may fear the unknown, while others are excited about the exploration of new worlds - to go where no one has gone before.

In the initial structuring there will be a strong commitment to the mission. The visionary leader

---

[5] https://www.youtube.com/watch?v=lAwhrLHsIGQ

communicates his vision and its significance. Many are attracted by its purpose. The leader's positive enthusiasm attracts others with positive and supportive attitudes. The future is still unclear but it does not dampen the enthusiasm of the followers. There is a mutual dependency as each – leader and followers – are willing to work long hours. In this phase, decision making is spontaneous, plans are being formulated and there is very little organizational structure. Because of this, people are receptive to change and it is easy to make course corrections. Everyone involved feels an ownership. Morale and self-esteem is high. Innovation and creativity thrive in new organizations.

Formal Organization,

After the initial startup, a more formal organization is normally established. This heightens the sense of mission and purpose among every member as they begin to understand their role in the group. They now begin to see the vision of the organization coming to fruition. This results in a high level of goal "ownership." People begin to give a high percentage of their time and identity to the organization. It is easy to get volunteers and new members or employees are excited to come aboard.

The organization's structural "form" is governed by "function." That means that the form of the structure is created only in response to the corporate functional needs. It is at this point that traditions begin to form, but it is still reasonably easy to incorporate changes and integrate them into the whole organization. Morale is still high and leaders consider suggestions from all levels. Self-esteem is easily affected by circumstances, short term successes, and failures.

Maximum Efficiency,

When the business has reached or is approaching "maximum efficiency," the mission and purpose are still highly visible and well understood by everyone within the organization. All participants or employees realize the common purpose and work together for its achievement. Even new people quickly find their place and participate enthusiastically. New programs are created to respond to new needs. Leaders freely delegate responsibility and authority and new roles are created. New proposals are given serious consideration. Morale and self-esteem are at their highest levels and confidence has become contagious.

Institutionalization,

When the organization reaches the institutionalization phase, there is a lowering of members understanding of its purpose. People begin to look only at their own small areas of responsibility and do not extend themselves to volunteer to help outside their limited tasks. The attitude has become, "I have done my thing, now there are enough others to do the new tasks."

Older members or employees feel they have done their part and do not need to take on new responsibilities. Few, if any, new programs are added. Now the organizational structure itself creates needs, rather than responding to needs. Changes, when proposed are not considered if they radically depart from the status quo. Morale becomes polarized into two groups; high and low. Self-esteem develops uncertainties.

Institutionalized organizations are commonly referred to as bureaucracies. The following quote comes from a "Tongue in Cheek" article by historian C. Northcote Parkinson. It appeared in the November 1955 edition of The Economist. Parkinson typifies an organization in the institutionalized phase.

> *"Granted that work (and especially paper work) is thus elastic in its demands on time, it is manifest that there need be little or no relationship between the work to be done and the size of the staff to which it may be assigned. Before the discovery of a new scientific law – herewith presented to the public for the first time, and*

15

to be called Parkinson's Law*— there has, however, been insufficient recognition of the implications of this fact in the field of public administration.[6]

Parkinson's Law roughly states,

"Work expands so as to fill the time available for its completion."

This is a good definition of "Institutionalization." Parkinson based his theory on studies of the British Admiralty over fourteen years from 1914 to 1928. In that period the number of capital ships in the fleet was reduced by sixty percent while the staff at headquarters increased seventy five percent. Parkinson actually created a mathematical formula predicting institutional growth of between five and seven percent per year, regardless of the amount of work required.

$$x = \frac{(2k^m + p)}{n}$$

Where: "x" is the number of new staff needed each year; "k" is the number of current staff seeking promotion through hiring new subordinates; "p" represents the difference between the age of appointment and retirement age; "m" is the number of man-hours devoted to responding to memos within the department; and "n" is the number of units overseen. The cost involved in this institutional expansion cannot be sustained and will ultimately lead to disintegration.

Disintegration

In the disintegration phase the organizational purpose is lost and mission not understood. Programs are eliminated for lack of participation. It is difficult to recruit new participants and/or employees. Ten percent of the workers are doing ninety percent of the work. Funding has become difficult and services

---

[6] C. Northcote Parkinson, November 19, 1955
http://www.economist.com/node/14116121

are being reduced or eliminated. The primary focus is on preservation and survival.

At one board meeting, I attended, the president made an announcement that the companies largest customer was undergoing a slowdown and their purchases would be reduced by ten percent. His solution was to raise his prices ten percent to compensate for the reduction in the number of parts the customer ordered. That same company had never produced a five year plan. When they were encouraged to plan ahead, the response was, "We've never done it that way before. We do not even know whether we will be here in five years."

In the disintegration phase, Leaders rationalize why goals cannot be achieved. Morale is at an all-time low. Leaders do not know how to stop the decline resulting in frustration and despair among workers whose self -esteem suffers.

Building to Last

Chapter 2 - Structure

Earlier we defined an organization as "an entity …that has a collective goal and is linked to an external environment." As we look at organizational development throughout the years, it is apparent that the external environment informs the organizational purpose, structure, and culture. An organization cannot exist to serve itself. When an organization exists to gratify itself, it will become institutionalized and later move into disintegration unless severe remedial measures are instituted.

Tracking the history of organizational development requires an understanding of the environment of the times. Organizations began at the time when humans first started gathering together in villages for protection. Civilization grew and city states were created. Still individual artisans created products and bartered or sold them in the market place. Eventually the Industrial Revolution transformed the single artisan into an organization. Now we have passed into "Modernism" and "Post Modernism." All of these environmental changes have impacted the way organizations interact with the environment. Organizational development follows and responds to the cultural, sociological, philosophical, and the technological environment.

Organizational structures are relatively new to civilization. Early "hunter-gatherers" were strictly loners, and had no need for organization. Relationships were tenuous at best as everyone was out for themselves, doing their own thing, and competing with one another to satisfy the physical needs of food shelter and safety. As humankind began to gather into small groups there was a need for cooperation. Cooperation required a form of organization and a set of rules for the betterment of the group. The top priority of the group was survival, which required a leader who was either the best fighter or the smartest in protecting the group. The

19

organization would include; fighters to protect the group from invasions by other groups, hunters who provide meat and animal skins for protection from the elements, and farmers who grew crops. Later as several groups came together forming villages, there arose a need for mutual support. Individuals with a talent for tanning animal skins and making clothes became the local tailor. Those who processed the field crops into food became millers and bakers. In the bronze and iron age a need arose for someone to forge plows, pots, and spears. Smithies began to create all types of metal tools and implements.

At this point in time, and well into the future, individual artisans produced products and commerce developed for food, clothing and implements. Each individual operated autonomously. The organization was the family unit; father, mother, and children. It was a hierarchal structure where father was in charge of the business, the mother had real authority and ran the household, and the children became the workers or employees. It was expected that the sons would continue the family business. Sons of millers, farmers, and smiths would become apprentices, learning the trade and carrying on the father's business.

Autonomous artisanal workers were still the primary mode of commerce through the eighteenth century. By 1820 eighty percent of the population of the United States was dependent on autonomous income while a mere twenty percent received wage income. As mobility and more efficient technology developed, self-sufficiency declined as sons and daughters found employment away from home in factories and businesses. By 1950, ninety percent of the population was supported by wage income, (income from employment by organizations.) Farmers, small shop owners, and skilled craftsmen made up the other ten percent of the workforce and were the only ones not dependent upon an organization for wages. As the nation's population grew and mobility was more available - with the development of the automobile, trucks and mass transit - the autonomous farmers and artisans struggled to support the demands of a growing population, causing individual and family production to be minimized in favor of the large and affluent organizations. Even farming was transformed into agro-business. At this time, elementary and secondary education grew out of the "one room" country school - once the purview of the local neighborhood – and consolidated into large organizations with multiple levels of management and specialization.

Mass media spread the word about the advantages of modernization. Economic development was spurred by new technologies and was supported by a more educated society. In the 1960's and 1970's there was an anti-modernism impetus against mass media and its evils.

Today we are in what has been referred to as "Post Modernism." This has been defined as a late 20th-century movement characterized by broad skepticism, subjectivism, relativism, a suspicion of reason, and an acute sensitivity to the role of ideology in asserting and maintaining political and economic power.

As organizations developed, several influential academics proposed and created experiments to determine the most efficient and productive management structures which would satisfy the need of the organization while successfully engaging with the organization's environment and purpose.

Even the church which began with groups of believers meeting secretly in homes in Israel and Asia Minor, then in the catacombs below Rome, became organized and integrated into the Roman Empire by Constantine. As reformers broke off from the Roman church, their followers grew and developed into denominations, which in turn grew into large organizations.

There is not a single way that is best to structure an organization, lead a company, or make decisions. The form of the structure is dependent upon the role of the organization, the organizational culture and the environment. Form should always follow function.

Rationalism/Newtonian

In her book, "Leadership and The New Science, Discovering Order in A Chaotic World" author Margaret J. Wheatley writes;

> *The universe that Sir Isaac Newton described was a seductive place. As the great clock ticked, we grew smart and designed the age of machines. As the pendulum swung with perfect periodicity, it prodded us on to new discoveries. As the Earth circled the sun (just like clockwork), we grew assured of the role of determinism and prediction. We absorbed expectations of regularity into our very beings. And we organized work and knowledge based on our beliefs about this predictable universe.*[7]

Early economic rationalists posited the existence of four distinct understandings of rationality - practical, theoretic, substantive, and formal.

1. Practical rationality starts by considering the final result, and then the individual decides on a systematic approach to achieve that result. It is a pragmatic way to achieve the desired result.

2. Theoretical rationality involves abstract concepts which will be essential to the element of logic. Theoretical models are used rather than the pragmatic approach. Today, with our computer

---

[7] Wheatley, Margaret J. (2006-09-01). Leadership and the New Science: Discovering Order in a Chaotic World (Kindle Locations 621-624). Berrett-Koehler Publishers. Kindle Edition.

modeling techniques, modeling has been greatly enhanced in economic and military war-fighting models using gaming techniques.

3. Substantive rationality involves the consideration of a range of values and actions which used to bring a cohesive plan together. Problems may arise when competing values cause deep divisions within the organization.

4. Formal rationality is a broader form of rationality that characterizes bureaucratic organizations. It sets up rules, laws and regulations that are uniformly applied even when the situation is different.

Bureaucracy

German sociologist, philosopher, and economist, "Max" Weber (1864 - 1920) influenced social theory, social research, and the entire discipline of sociology. He feared that formal rationality was taking over western society and as substantive rationality declined it would lead to the elimination of other forms of rationality, limiting creative social action.

Weber wrote about the emergence of bureaucracy and its growing popularity in modern society. He proposed that an ideal bureaucracy consists of six specific characteristics:[8]

- Hierarchy of command: Subordinates follow orders of superiors, but have right of appeal (in contrast to more diffuse structure in traditional authority).

- Impersonality: Officials are selected on basis of technical qualifications, appointed not elected, and compensated by salary.

---

[8] Dobbin, Frank. "The Rise of Bureaucracy." Harvard University. Harvard Hall, Cambridge, MA. 12 September 2012.

- Written rules of conduct: Intentional, abstract rules govern decisions and actions. Rules are stable, exhaustive, and can be learned. Decisions are recorded in permanent files.

- Advancement based on achievement:

- Specialized division of labor: Jurisdictional areas are clearly specified, activities are distributed as official duties.

- And efficiency.

Efficiency was the ultimate characteristic of a Weberian bureaucracy. However, Parkinson demonstrates that bureaucracies become inefficient when they lose sight of their purpose and workload, and seek to grow for growth sake. Weber's view of bureaucracy was a system of power where leaders exercise control over others based primarily on position and discipline. Weber did have a serious concern about expanding state bureaucracies and considered how this could be restricted by society. His concern was mismanagement and inefficiency as the power of public officials increased. [9]

Scientific Management

In a rational organization system, there are two significant parts: Specificity of Goals and Formalization. Goal specification provides guidelines for specific tasks to be completed along with a regulated way for resources to be allocated. Formalization is a way to standardize organizational behavior. As a result, there will be stable expectations, which create the rational organizational system. [10]

---

[9] Weber, Max. Economy and Society: An Outline of Interpretive Sociology (2 Volume Set). University of California Press.

[10] Taylor, Frederick. Scientific Management

Scientific management, also called Taylorism, is a theory of management whose main goal is to analyze the work process and develop practices to improve efficiency of labor, thereby increasing productivity. It applied scientific method to management and production engineering. It began with Frederick Winslow Taylor (1856-1915) in the 1880's and 1890's. Taylor was a Mechanical Engineer in the United States and one of the first efficiency experts. He summed up his efficiency techniques in his book "The Principles of Scientific Management." Taylor analyzed how to maximize the amount of output with the least amount of input. This was Taylor's attempt to rationalize the individual worker. The elements of Taylorism consisted of:

- Division of work between managers and workers.

- Incentive systems based on performance.

- Scientifically trained workers.

- Creation of scientific explanation for each individual's responsibilities.

- Ensuring that work is accomplished on time and efficiently.

Scientific management became most influential in manufacturing in the 1910's then its importance waned in the 1920's. Although scientific management as a distinct school of thought was obsolete by the 1930s, most of its themes are still important parts of Industrial Engineering and management today.

This was still in vogue in the 1950' and 1960's in some industries. Several problems arose in Taylor's method. Standardization of processes led to a mundaneness which reduced worker's morale, often leading to rebellion. Workers objected to the incentive system because they were required to constantly work at their optimum level, an expectation they considered unrealistic.

Division of Labor

Adam Smith, (1723-1790) Scottish moral philosopher, pioneer of political economy, and key Scottish enlightenment figure wrote the classic, *"An Inquiry into the Nature and Causes of the Wealth of Nations,"* which was published in 1776. In Book 1, Smith wrote about an organizational style he called the "Division of Labour."

> *"Division of labour has caused a greater increase in production than any other factor. This diversification is greatest for nations with more industry and improvement, and is responsible for "universal opulence" in those countries. Agriculture is less amenable than industry to division of labour; hence, rich nations are not so far ahead of poor nations in agriculture as in industry."*

Smith was also quoted as writing:

> *"Division of labour arises not from innate wisdom, but from humans' propensity to barter. The apparent difference in natural talents between people is a result of specializations, rather than any innate cause."*

"The real price of everything," says Adam Smith[11] "What everything really costs to the man who wants to acquire it, is the toil and trouble of acquiring it. What everything is really worth to the man who has acquired it, and who wants to dispose of it, or exchange it for something else, is the toil and trouble which it can save to himself, and which it can impose upon other people. That this is really the foundation of the exchangeable value of all things, excepting those which cannot be increased by human industry, is a doctrine of the utmost importance in political economy."

---

[11]   Smith, A., 1976, The Wealth of Nations edited by R.H. Campbell and A.S. Skinner, The Glasgow edition of the Works and Correspondence of Adam Smith, vol. 2b, pp. 47

According to Adam Smith the division of labor is efficient because:

1. Occupational specialization develops more efficient workers as repetition improves speed and accuracy;

2. It provides a saving from not changing tasks;

3. And machines can take the place of human labor.

Occupational specialization leads to increased productivity and distinct skill. Also, Smith argued that human and physical capital must be similar or matched. If the skill of workers were matched with technological improvements, there would be a major increase in productivity.

There were many critics of Smith's organizational theory. Alfred Marshal argued that man should be more important than money, services are more important than goods; the emphasis should be placed on human welfare instead of wealth. These arguments seem as if they were torn from today's headlines.

Modernism

Modernization theory in organizational development involves the transition from traditional methods of organizing to pursue more contemporary, effective methods. With the increase in population there comes a larger demand for a capable workforce.

The growth of modernization took place beginning in the 1950s. For the ensuing decade, people analyzed the diffusion of technological innovations within Western society and the communication that helped it disperse globally. This first "wave" as it became known had some significant ramifications. First, economic development was enhanced from the spread of new technological techniques. And second, modernization supported a more educated society, and thus a more qualified labor force.

27

The second wave took place between the years 1960 and 1970. This period was labeled anti-modernization, because it saw the push of innovations of Western society onto developing countries as an exertion of dominance. It refuted the concept of relying heavily on mass media for the betterment of society.

Frank Dobbins writes,

"Although this theory of modernization seemed to pride itself on only the benefits, countries in the Middle East saw this movement in a new light. Middle Eastern countries believed that the media coverage of modernization implied that the more traditional societies have not risen to a higher level of technological development. Consequently, they believed a movement that benefits those who have the monetary resources to modernize technological development would discriminate against the minorities and poor masses. Thus, they were reluctant to modernize because of the economic gap it would create between the rich and the poor."[12]

The last wave of modernization theory, which took place in the 1990s, depicts impersonality. As uses of newspapers, TVs, and radios become more prevalent, the need for direct contact, a concept traditional organizations took pride in, diminishes. Thus, organizational interactions become more distant.

"Modern institutions are transparently purposive and that we are in the midst an evolutionary progression towards more efficient forms." [Dobbin]

This phrase is typical of the vision of modern corporations, bureaucracies, and organizations. Technology and innovation have become the source for reaching the end

---

[12] Dobbin, Frank (1994). Cultural Models of Organization: The Social Construction of Rational Organizing Principles. Oxford: Basil Blackwell.

goals. In this environment, the main goal of organizations is to survive. If they are to survive they do more than maintain a profitable bottom line. They must develop legitimate reputations internationally.

> *"Transcendental economic laws exist, that existing organizational structures must be functional under the parameters of those laws, [and] that the environment will eliminate organizations that adopt non-efficient solutions" [Dobbin]*[13]

These laws lead modern organizations to maximize profits efficiently. This is the priority of the modern organizations that uses mass media advertising, technological innovations and social innovations in order to allocate resources for improving their environment – the global economy.

Postmodern

Post modernism emerged out of a rejection of modernism. Modernism promised a Utopian world with all problems solved by rationality, science, finances, and hard work. The attitude was, "Put it all together and nothing can stand in the way of progress." With the tremendous growth of knowledge in physics, psychology, and sociology the problems of the world remain unsolved. And, in the minds of many the existing problems seem to be growing worse while new problems arise. Post Modernism is characterized by relativism, distrust of scientific method, and distrust of authority. A major result of the post-modern culture is the growth of "Tribalism". This term is commonly used today in popular literature and reflects a tribal consciousness and loyalty, exaltation of the tribe above other groups, and strong in-group loyalty.

A "Tribe" can be defined as,

---

[13] IBID pp138

Building to Last
A social group comprising numerous families, clans, or generations together, a political: a group of persons having a common character, occupation, or interest.[14]

While "Tribalism" is defined as:

Tribal consciousness and loyalty; esp : exaltation of the tribe above other groups; strong in-group loyalty

One of the effects of tribalism can be seen in the geo-political arena where nations are splitting apart forming two or more individual nations (tribes). The former USSR was broken into several independent states. Germany was re-united into one tribe. The Czech Republic and Slovakia came out of the former Czechoslovakia. The Muslim nations are dividing between Islamic sects. Even in the United States, we see greater divisions between races and immigrant societies. Rather than becoming assimilated into the culture where they now live, people are maintaining their own tribal language and culture. This is not meant to be a criticism, only a commentary. This is the environment of the Post Modern era. This is the environment with which our organizations must interact. Above all of this tribalism is reflected in the inability of political parties to come together to solve the nation's problems. The tribes, Democrat and Republican, seem more important than the USA.

In her book *"The Future and Its Enemies, The Growing Conflict over Creativity, Enterprise and Progress"* author Virginia Postrel[15] wrote in 1998 that a major battle was forming for the future of the nation. Postrel contends that the battle for control of the future was not between opposing tribes, liberals and conservatives, nor between nations. The battle is between

---

[14]   Merriam-Webster (2009-06-12). Merriam-Webster's Collegiate Dictionary, 11th Edition (Kindle Locations 605557-605558). Merriam-Webster, Inc.. Kindle Edition

[15]   Postrel, Virginia, The Future and its Enemies, the Growing Conflict Over Creativity, Enterprise, And Progress, The Free Press, Div. of Simon & Schuster, NY, NY 1998

"Dynamists" and "Stasists." The author uses the term Dynamism," to refer not just to change, but evolution through variation, feedback, and adaption." It is the trial and error method. Dynamists are not afraid to make mistakes because they grow from their mistakes as a learning process. There is spontaneity and wild abandon in dynamism. When mistakes are made, they can be corrected and then you can make progress. Creativity flourishes in this environment.

Stasists, on the other hand, feel that they must control progress –establish rules and regulations to ensure safety and avoid mistakes. We see government agencies establishing rules and regulations which inhibit creativity and business growth. They are putting requirements on everything from industry operations to the food we eat. In the church stasists would be the Pharisees and legalists.

Postrel holds up the internet as an example of what can be accomplished when there is minimal control. Tremendous technological progress - without control - has led to a huge volume of information available to everyone and the cost of communications around the world is significantly reduced. But without controls there are problems. As a result we have pornography, terrorists plotting, and hacking of intellectual property. Creativity flourishes without control. Control inhibits creativity, but it is safer.

> *"The future we face at the dawn of the twenty-first century is, like all futures left to themselves, "emergent, complex messiness." Its "messiness" lies not in disorder, but in an order that is unpredictable, spontaneous, and ever shifting, a pattern created by millions of uncoordinated, independent decisions. That pattern contains not just a few high-tech gizmos, but all the variegated aspects of life. As people create and sell products or services, adopt new fashions of speech or dress, form families and choose home towns, make medical decisions and seek spiritual insights,*

31

investigate the universe and invent new forms of art, these actions shape a future no one can see, a future that is dynamic and inherently unstable."[16]

While in the military industrial environment, I learned that there was a distinct difference in the procurement practices for major weapons systems by different military agencies. One group established performance criteria and allowed contractors leeway in design to meet the criteria, while another military agency provided a rigorous design package complete down to the minutest detail. They asked companies to bid on producing the exact design. The latter could be in the stasist philosophy while the former would lean more to the dynamist. Static or dynamic are the derivations of these categories.

We have entered into a most creative time period inn all of history, but we must realize that creativity results in change and change is disruptive to the normal flow. Conflicts erupt wherever change exists.

In our postmodern world the way in which we organize and manage has changed with not only our changing society, but in the products which we offer. Our economy is no longer based primarily on natural resources, farming and manufacturing. Instead our economy is substantially service oriented. Service is relational therefore relationships play a larger role than the hierarchal structure.

Relational

At the end of World War II, the automotive industry of the United States was converting factories from war production to consumer vehicles. During the war our War Department had imposed strict quality assurance procedures on all manufacturers of weapons systems in an effort to assure quality and interchangeability of parts. As a result our nation's ability to produce masses of guns, tanks, jeeps and airplanes

---

[16] IBID "Introduction"

was a major factor in defeating our invaders. A form of statistical quality assurance was developed and implemented in a large part by William Edwards Deming (1900 - 1993). After the war, auto manufacturers returned to the production of civilian vehicles and felt that they no longer required the strict War Department regulations and reverted to prewar practices.

Demming was no longer need in Detroit. Oceans away the Japanese, realizing that their reputation of poor quality was hurting their fledgling auto and electronics industries were open to suggestions by Americas quality expert. There in August 1950 at the Hakone Convention Center in Tokyo, Deming delivered a seminal speech on what he called Statistical Product Quality Administration. Deming was the inspiration for what has since become known as the Japanese post-war economic miracle of 1950 to 1960. In those years Japan rose from the ashes of war to become the second most powerful economy in the world in less than a decade. This transformation was founded on the ideas Deming taught:[17]

- The problems facing manufacturers can be solved through cooperation, despite differences.

- Marketing is not sales. It is the science of knowing what repeat customers think of a product, as well as whether, and why, they will buy it again.

- Initial stages of design must include market research, applying statistical techniques for planning and inspecting samples.

- The manufacturing process must be perfected.

A biographical sketch of Demming is quoted directly from the Website www.managementwisdom.com the bold emphasis was not in the original but was inserted here by the author.

---

[17] Deming's 1950 Lecture to Japanese Management . Translation by Teruhide Haga. Accessed: 2011-07-10.

*Raised on the Wyoming frontier in a poor family, Deming experienced hardship and **learned early about cooperation as a way of life**. He saw the value of shared benefits in barn raisings, quilting bees and advice to sugar beet farmers from the Great Western Sugar Company.*

*Deming was educated in engineering and physics and became an early **student of statistics, the theory of knowledge** and **systems thinking**. He eventually integrated the disciplines of statistical thinking, how people learn, systems thinking and psychology into his theory of profound knowledge, which allows leaders and managers to see a dynamic, complex social system in new ways, predict its performance, and continually improve it in a rapidly changing world. **Using his ideas to eliminate cross-purposes, teams and organizations can produce greater wholes — more than any of the individual parts or people added together can.***

*His work has been called the **third wave of the industrial revolution after the steam engine and the production line**. In a 1991 cover story, **US News & World Report listed Deming's philosophy, along with St. Paul, the numerous pre-Columbian discoveries of America, and Napoleon's conquest of Europe, as one of history's nine hidden turning points.***

*Deming would evoke disbelief in his management seminars when he insisted that **94 percent or more of all problems, defective goods or services came from the system, not from a careless worker or a defective machine**. He would go on to say that to improve an organization's goods or services, the system had to be improved rather than searching for the guilty worker or broken equipment. Top managers in America's leading companies were dubious*

34

students. But, in almost all cases, when they implemented his ideas, they were surprised to find that they agreed with him: The management and the system they were managing were the true source of both problems and improvements.

*In the years since its introduction, Deming's philosophy of continual improvement of products, services, processes, systems and people has rarely been practiced in its fullness. In too many cases, his philosophical principles have been reduced to promoting only continual improvement in products and services to please or delight customers. Instead of focusing on the more intangible aspects of his philosophy, as Deming advised, **American companies have focused almost exclusively on the tangible products and services produced by those systems. They have often substituted measurement for management.** As a result of this linear-minded focus on the tangible outcomes, Deming's goal of the complete transformation of organizations and their people remains an opportunity waiting in the wings, but we have no doubt that it will someday be as universally accepted as the assembly line.*

We have devoted considerable space to Deming and his accomplishments because he was so far ahead of his time. His ideas inspired Japanese executives to initiate reforms in their organizations which transformed their companies. Japan, once the butt of jokes about poorly manufactured parts, became the reliability standard for the world in manufacturing. One of the first changes they made was to institute "Quality Circles," where workers and managers involved in the manufacturing process met together regularly to discuss and implement methods to improve the processes.

Deming's first item on the list of ideas was cooperative problem solving which has become the cornerstone of the movement from "Hierarchal" organizations to "Relational" organizations.

Margaret Wheatley[18] compares hierarchal organizations with other living organisms and writes,

> *"We need to stop seeking after the universe of the seventeenth century and begin to explore what has become known to us during the twentieth century. We need to expand our search for the principles of organization to include what is presently known about how the universe organizes."*

As we look at what science has discovered about the universe as well as a tiny drop of water, it all appears to be organized the same. The universe contains galaxies of stars, stars have solar systems, and planets have moons. Each is connected to the other by invisible fields and quanta of energy. Everything we feel and touch is organized in the same manner. A chair is made up of molecules held together by invisible forces. The molecules consist of atoms electrons, protons and neutrons. Then there are quarks and leptons.

Wheatley points out; relationships in the scientific life should be considered also for organizational life.

> *There are many attempts to leave behind the view that predominated in the twentieth century, when we believed that organizations could succeed by confining workers to narrow roles and asking only for very partial contributions. As we let go of the machine model of organizations, and workers as replaceable cogs in the machinery of production, we begin to see ourselves in much richer dimensions, to appreciate our wholeness, and, hopefully, to design organizations that*

---

[18] Wheatley, Margaret J. (2006-09-01). Leadership and the New Science: Discovering Order in a Chaotic World (Kindle Locations 144-145). Berrett-Koehler Publishers. Kindle Edition.

honor and make use of the great gift of who we humans are.

.........Scientists in many different disciplines are questioning whether we can adequately explain how the world works by using the machine imagery emphasized in the seventeenth century by such great geniuses as Sir Isaac Newton and René Descartes.

First, I don't believe that organizations are ever changed by imposing a model developed elsewhere. So little transfers to, or inspires, those trying to work at change in their own organizations. In every organization, we need to look internally, to see one another as the critical resources on this voyage of discovery.

How do we create structures that are flexible and adaptive, that enable rather than constrain? How do we simplify things without losing what we value about complexity? How do we resolve personal needs for autonomy and growth with organizational needs for prediction and accountability?

Authors Ori Brafman and Rod A. Beckstrom, explore the phenomena of decentralization in their 2008 book, The Starfish and the Spider, the Unstoppable Power of Leaderless Organizations.

"A leaderless organization is one which is completely and totally decentralized. People remain part of one because they subscribe to its underlying philosophy rather than due to any contractual or formal arrangements. There are no entry requirements to join a leaderless organization and nobody actually owns it or makes money from it overtly. In all, leaderless organizations are an entirely different kind of way to structure a business which would be easy to dismiss as

being only hypothetical if it wasn't for the fact they are becoming more common and more successful." [19]

A few examples of successful decentralized organizations are:

Skype: Skype is a next-generation phone company which uses the Internet rather than telephone lines. The company has no central servers or big offices. Instead, users download free software and plug a headset into their PC. EBay acquired Skype for $4.1 billion.

Craigslist: In 1995, Craig Newmark started a Web site to keep track of local San Francisco Bay area events. More and more people started posting to his list until today it features small free-format classified ads for 175 cities around the world. It is estimated that Craigslist generates around $10 million a year that way. The entire project is self-regulating – anyone is free to post whatever they like but if something is offensive, other users can remove the ad.

Alcoholics Anonymous: This is probably the most well-known decentralized organization of all. The founder of AA was Bill Wilson who was told he needed to stop drinking in 1935. He realized he couldn't combat alcoholism by himself so Bill decided to enlist the help of others who were in the same predicament as he. AA was formed to help alcoholics to help themselves quit.

"In the digital world, decentralization will continue to change the face of industry and society. Fighting these forces of change is at best futile and at worst counterproductive. But these same forces can be harnessed for immense power: just ask the music-swappers, the Skype callers, the eBay merchants, the Wikipedia contributors, the Craigslist community

---

[19]   Ori Brafman and Rod A. Beckstrom , *The Starfish and the Spider, The unstoppable power of leaderless organizations*. 2008, Penguin Group

members, the recovering addicts, or anyone who's ever used the Internet.[20]

The authors continue, "Like starfish, decentralized organizations stand on five legs:

- Circles which are independent and autonomous.

- A catalyst who initiates a circle

- An underlying ideology

- A preexisting network which can be accessed.

- A champion who gets things done."

Decentralized organizations can function alright without one or two of these legs but when all five are working together, the organization can really take off. Branfman and Beckstrom contrast the way CEO driven organizations with a "Catalyst" driven organizations. It is good to remember that "Catalysts are agents of change.

Decentralized organizations can function alright without one or two of these legs but when all five are working together, the organization can really take off. Branfman and Beckstrom contrast the way CEO driven organizations with a "Catalyst" driven organizations. It is good to remember that "Catalysts are agents of change.

CEO Driven	*Catalyst Driven*
Boss	A Peer
Command & Control	Draws on trust
Rational	Emotional and smart

---

[20] Publishing, BusinessNews (2014-10-14). Summary : The Starfish and the Spider - Ori Brafman and Rod Beckstrom: The Unstoppable Power of Leaderless Organizations (Kindle Locations 180-184). Must Read Summaries. Kindle Edition

Powerful	Inspirational
Gives directives	More collaborative
Always in the spotlight	Behind the scenes
Highly Structured	More ambiguous
Spends time organizing and strategizing.	Usually found connecting with others

Decentralized organizations at first glance appear to be messy and chaotic.

Hierarchical Newtonian model	Organic Relational Model
Efficiency is the most important issue	Effectiveness is most important issue
Replication of tasks (organizationally)	Develop Relationships
Rigid Goals	Creativity
Spend time at work (8 hours days)	Innovative space – time to contemplate
Facts are most important	Information is vital
Speed	Results
Authority derived from position	Favor/recognized authority
Top Down Management	Propagation -
Pre-Specified Success	Post Specified Success – Inspect the fruit
Decisions are final	Iterative Process
Predicted results	Surprises & Delight
Engineered future	Cultivated change
Designed authority	Emergent Identity

Centralized anointing	Power of many
Long term sustainability	Tactical advancement
Responsibility to others	Experience with others
Honoring heritage	Breaking down traditions
Accountability	Anointing to serve
Name Recognition	Impact Identity
Change is an interruption	Change is life
Fixed five year plan	Progressive plan
Homogeneous Policies	Heterogeneous practices
Equilibrium is desired	Equilibrium is transitory
Managed outcome	Managed mindset
Predictable results	Anticipated results
Directed strategies	Emergent strategies

In our postmodern world the way in which we organize and manage has changed with not only our changing society, but in the products which we offer. Our economy is no longer based primarily on natural resources, farming and manufacturing. Instead our economy is substantially service oriented. Service is relational therefore relationships play a larger role than the hierarchal structure.

Chapter 3 - Culture

As national marketing manager for an electronic components manufacturer dealing around the country, I realized a great difference in business practices and relationships of the different companies with which I dealt. Coming from a conservative Midwest background, I anticipated that attitudes and business practices in other regions would be different, but I did not realize how different. Beyond regional differences, there were strong variations in even within geographical areas. Some customers were courteous while others treated us poorly and with disrespect. Some were kind, encouraging, accepting, and considerate, while others acted as if you were bothering them. We wrongly assumed that the discourteous ones just did not like sales people bothering them. Later, while employed by a major systems integrator, I was on the other side dealing those same companies as their customer. This time they were selling to me, but their attitudes were identical to how we were treated as a supplier. The people we dealt with were different but their attitudes and business methods were consistent throughout the organization. This was demonstrated from the highest corporate officers down to the workers on the manufacturing floor. There was a distinct culture built into every organization that permeates throughout.

John Kotter, Professor of Leadership emeritus at Harvard Business School defines culture;

> *"Culture consists of group norms of behavior and the underlying shared values that help keep those norms in place. Take your work, for example, a place where almost everyone shows up between 8:55 and 9:05. Why? Not because the CEO has decreed it, or because people are fired if they don't do it. That's just the way it is! That is a group norm. Why does it exist? And why doesn't it go away when Gen X or Y individuals*

are hired? My guess: People are hired who embrace the value of respecting others, including other people's time, so they also show up to meetings on time, and anyone who doesn't gets a glaring look from everyone else.[21]

Organizational culture originates at conception and reflects the values, priorities, and practices of the founder(s). It becomes set in the organizations DNA. In my experience dealing with hundreds of different organizations, both for-profit and non-profit, churches and industries, all have a distinctive culture and personality that is reflected in their inherent values, priorities and practices.

In order to better explain these phenomena, it is helpful to visualize a new building under construction. This provides a reasonable metaphor for building an organization from the ground up. As there are many types of organizations, there are many types of buildings, each constructed to fulfill an objective or purpose; church, school, hospital, office, factory, etc. The facility used to achieving that purpose may look different in specific situations. The building, or the organization, does not exist in a vacuum. It will operate within and interact with their environment. The organization's values, priorities, and practices will define the culture and the manner of interaction with that environment.

Values

Values are unseen but influential. Values are like the excavation within which the foundation of a superstructure is placed. Values set the location and the limits of activities. They are there but out of view.

---

[21]   http://www.forbes.com/sites/johnkotter/2012/09/27/the-key-to-changing-organizational-culture/

You do not think about values but they affect what you think, and as a result, what you do.[22]

The first step in constructing a new building or facility is site selection and excavation of the foundation. As our company expanded into new products and technologies, we wanted to be close to potential customers in Southern California. In Anaheim, we selected a site adjacent to that of a company with whom we had often partnered together on several projects. We acquired the land on a ninety nine year lease and selected the building contractor. We watched as a former avocado grove was cleared, graded, and the foundation laid for the erection of an engineering laboratory and manufacturing plant. Excavating to lay the foundation was the first step in the construction process. This is likened to the value system of the organization.

Organizations founded on defective values - personal, corporate, or societal - will result in faulty foundations and will lead to fracturing or failure of the organization. We have seen ministries that were founded because of a divisive church suffer the same fate, dying in a divisive split. When the organization is founded in conflict it too will suffer conflict.

Several years ago while living in Ridgeland, Mississippi, we were introduced to a type of soil called "Yazoo Clay"[23] which has the capability to absorb large amounts of water. As a result foundations have a tendency to float around and become unstable. We watched as one house in our neighborhood developed large cracks in the walls and eventually led to the house splitting in half. Then one day we watched as foundation repair crews worked on the house directly across the street.

---

[22] Wimber, John "Building a Church From the Bottom Up" Church Planting Seminar, February, 1993, Anaheim Vineyard

[23] Stover, Curtis W. Yazoo Clay, Engineering Aspects and Environmental Geology of an Expansive Clay, Mississippi Department of Natural Resources, Bureau of Geology, Jackson MS, 1988

They had to re-excavate the foundation to prevent the carport from breaking free from the house. That is the problem with building a house on Yazoo clay.

The city of New Orleans is built on the silt build-up in the delta of the Mississippi River. Erosion of Midwestern soil brought rich soil all the way down river where it settled and created land in what was once the Gulf of Mexico. Until the 1960's the maximum building heights were only three or four stories. Engineers then decided that they could drill down through the silt to bedrock using concrete and steel pilings to build taller buildings.

Organizational values must be strong enough, deep enough, and stable enough for the organization to grow beyond the limitations of the environment. While soil exaction and preparation is not seen in the building or to outsiders these conditions determine the ultimate size, effectiveness, and longevity of the resulting organization - business, church, or sports team.

The subject of core values has become a popular topic in business and organizational literature over recent years. Values determine what we do, how we will act, and how we react in all situations. Most of our identity revolves around the things that are most valuable to us. Values describe the beliefs of an individual or culture. They subjective and vary widely across individuals and organizations. They may include ethical/moral values, doctrinal/ideological values, social values, and aesthetic values.

Personal values are related to choice. They guide decisions by allowing for an individual to make choices. Personal values are developed early in life and are usually resistant to change. They normally are derived from particular groups or systems, such as society, religion, and/or political party. However, personal values are not universal; one's genes, family, nation, and history help determine one's personal values. Each individual possesses a unique conception of their

46

own values i.e. a personal knowledge of the appropriate values for their own genes, feelings, and experience.

Groups, societies, or cultures have values that are largely shared by their members. Members take part in an organization's value system even if each member's personal values do not entirely agree with some of the values sanctioned in the organization. This is reflected in an individual's ability to select from the multiple subcultures to which they belong. If a group member expresses a value that is in serious conflict with the group's values, the group's authority may carry out various ways of encouraging conformity or stigmatizing the non-conforming behavior of its members.

In his book, "Outliers: The Story of Success," Malcolm Gladwell cites studies which demonstrated that regional cultures in the United States could be attributed to the heritage and culture of the region's first settlers.

> *Cultural legacies are powerful forces. They have deep roots and long lives. They persist, generation after generation, virtually intact, even as the economic and social and demographic conditions that spawned them have vanished, and they play such a role in directing attitudes and behavior that we cannot make sense of our world without them.* [24]

As in the building analogy, the first thing established in any organization is its set of core values. They include the personal values held by the church planter or entrepreneur, the corporate values of a parent organization, and the cultural values of the nation or region of the country.

Values by themselves are hidden in the foundation and are not visible outside of the organization and often are not even seen by members or employees. The quality of the

---

[24] Gladwell, Malcolm (2008-10-29). Outliers: The Story of Success (p. 175). Little, Brown and Company.

building excavation is concealed but its effect on the structure now and in the future is substantial.

Values are difficult to change. They are embedded in the psyche of individuals and organizations. It will take a paradigm shift or catastrophic event, such as the collapse of a building or organization to change the value system. They are part of the organization's DNA, programmed in at start-up.

Values will dictate the organization's priorities, therefore it is important to identify the organization's values, not to change them, but to understand what drives the organization.

A quick exercise would be to look at the list of possible values listed below and prioritize your values by designating them (1) through (5) in their adjacent column. You are free to add other values that are significant to you.

Examples of some possible values are offered below:

Acceptance		Accountable		Action-Oriented		Ambitious	
Approachable		Attractiveness		Authority		Balance	
Boldness		Challenging		Caring		Commitment	
Compassion		Competence		Confidence		Confrontational	
Consistent		Contentment		Conviction		Cooperation	
Creativity		Credibility		Curious		Cutting Edge	
Decisive		Dedication		Determined		Diligence	
Effective		Empower		Encourage		Enthusiastic	
Entrepreneurial		Equality		Example		Excellence	
Family-Oriented		Faithful		Goal Oriented		Growth	
Happy		Healthy		Helpful		High Energy	
Honesty		Hope		Humility		Imagination	
Innovation		Integrity		Leadership		Love	
Maturity		Mercy		Nurture		Obedience	
Orderly		Organized		Passion		Patience	
Peace		People-oriented		Persistence		Positive	
Proactive		Problem solving		Progressive		Relationships	
Reliability		Reputation		Respectability		Responsiveness	
Teamwork		Thorough		Trustworthy		Visionary	

Priorities

For many of us a ringing telephone grabs our attention and it becomes our number one priority to respond. We have all experienced the cell phone alerting us of an incoming call as it imposes itself into our focus. We stop our work to answer and find it is either a wrong number or a telemarketer with the latest service we cannot do without. There is urgency about a phone ringing that says, "Quick, answer, it may be important."

> *"Most of us spend too much time on what is urgent and not enough time on what is important."* [Stephen R. Covey]

A "priority" is: Something given or meriting attention before competing alternatives.[25]

Priorities are the elements that give shape and limitation to the organization. Using our building metaphor, priorities are like pillars that set the edge of the value boundary. They would be the walls ceiling and floor. They grow out of the values but are more visible. They give a visible form to the values. Priorities are corporate convictions of the group. Priorities can be changed, but first values have to change, which we know is often difficult. Priorities accurately communicate the values of the group.

Different types of business organizations will have a different set of priorities. In most businesses profitability is a high priority, but "Not-For-Profit" organizations tend to have more altruistic priorities, while they do require financial support so they will always make raising support a high priority. For-Profit organizations have a responsibility to provide their stockholders with a return on their investment. But there are other priorities to consider. Corporations have a

---

[25] Merriam-Webster (2009-06-12). Merriam-Webster's Collegiate Dictionary, 11th Edition (Kindle Location 457462). Merriam-Webster, Inc.. Kindle Edition.

responsibility, not only to their stockholders, but also to their employees, customers, and their environment.

Our world has recently been through an economic downturn which continues to threaten the economies of several nations. The causes of the downturn are quite complex, but one factor stands out which led to this collapse - the over-emphasis on immediate financial returns over sustainability and growth. Several CEO's are currently serving time in penitentiaries due to illegal or immoral business practices that were used to hide the true financial condition of their companies. These practices resulted from the priority of increasing profits at all cost, which was a result of the value placed upon both corporate and individual wealth. When the top priority of any individual or organization becomes immediate financial reward, collapse is inevitable. When sustainability and growth are sacrificed there will always be a day of reckoning.

The West Coast Division of a Washington DC based corporation had developed a strong and stable team of engineers, technicians, and administrative staff effectively supporting its customers. The division grew rapidly and overhead remained the lowest of any of the divisions. As the entire company continued to grow, the board of directors began to look at potential merger candidates. Soon the company was merged into a corporation three times its size with a different set of values and priorities.

No visible change was immediately apparent except at corporate headquarters. But as time passed the entire company began to change as the culture, values, priorities, and practices of the surviving company began to permeate through the organization. Before the merger, the company had a family atmosphere. Employees were treated as part of the family – turkeys given at Thanksgiving and bonuses at Christmas. A priority was recruiting and keeping excellent employees.

At the time of the merger, the smaller company's profits exceeded those of the larger merger partner. The priorities of the merged corporation were focused more on immediate financial return. Employees became replaceable assets. The priority set on immediate profits became detriment to future growth. First, the turkeys stopped coming, then the bonuses. The bonus pool stayed the same, but after the merger, only top management participated. Pressure was exerted to continually exceed the previous year's numbers. Since then the organization has gone through several mergers, acquisitions and spinoffs and today does not exist as it once did.

The establishment of priorities is based upon the values of the organization. If immediate financial return is the reason the company was founded, it has the highest value and will be reflected in the priorities.

Jeff Bezos, the founder of Amazon, Inc. read a report on the future of the Internet. He noted that conducting business via the Web was predicted to have a phenomenal growth rate. After considering different products, he settled on providing an on-line book store. His first building was his garage in Bellevue, Washington. Within two months, Amazon's sales were up to twenty thousand dollars per week. Bezos' business plan for Amazon did not include immediate profitability. That was not a priority. In fact Amazon did not show a profit for four years and then only one cent per share on revenues of more than five billion dollars. As many of the Internet marketing businesses failed when the "dot-com" bubble burst in early 2000, Bezos' priority of establishing a strong organization ahead of instant returns allowed Amazon to succeed while other Internet enterprises fell. Today Amazon has become the major on-line retailer with a huge volume. Still the profit margin remains low for on-line marketing, but they continue to thrive with product lines and customer loyalty second to none.

It is significant to remember that an organization's priorities reflect the values of the organization. Priorities can only be changed when the values change.

Building to Last

Most organizations will state their priorities as part of a business plan but their priorities must be translated into action or "Practices"

Continuing with the "building" metaphor the "Practices" of an organization compare with the building's infrastructure. Within the walls are plumbing pipes, wires for electricity and communications, and heating and air conditioning ducts. Again these are not seen but their influence is felt. The practices of the organization are a function of the priorities. The organization's original intent when created reflects the values and priorities of the founders. The practices reflect the skills and passion which are the driving force of the organization.

"Action expresses priorities." (Mahatma Gandhi)

Some of the organizational practices would include, communications, business strategy, and dealing with employees, customers, and vendors.

Entrepreneurs often start companies for the intrinsic benefits of autonomy, significance and self-fulfillment. Others do it for the extrinsic rewards of money and fame. The latter category is in the minority and those founders often tire of the burden and quit or sell out.

The earlier example of the Washington D.C. based technical services company provided an example of the effect of changing values and priorities resulting in changed practices. The impetus for founding the first company was to fulfill a need was not being adequately served. This became the top priority. In order to fulfill the commitment to the customer the staff had to be the best available. Therefore the second priority was to recruit and maintain the best team available. As a result salaries and employee benefits had to be more than competitive. Later when the company was merged into a larger organization with a different values and priorities, the practices changed dramatically and the corporate culture also changed.

A comparison of practices before and after the merger shows how practices change when values and priorities change.

	Before Merger	After Merger
Priority	Serving the customer.	Serving the Organization.
Employee Practices	Employees were valued. Vacation, sick leave, gifts, and bonuses were liberally distributed.	Employees became resources for exploitation.
Management Style	Catalytic: Cooperative decision making.	Hierarchal and remote.
Life Cycle	Maximum Efficiency	Institutionalized

Practices

Practices are the principle help, or hindrance to organizational growth. Practices can be changed but first you have to work on the values and priorities.

In the building metaphor, Personnel are all the people who labor in the building, bounded by the values, supported by the priorities, and sustained by the practices. They are the people committed to the organization, trained in its practices, committed to its values, and priorities.

Finishing up on our building metaphor, programs are like rooms and corridors in the structure. Programs are not permanent like values, priorities, and practices. Outsiders see only the personnel and the programs. Programs are easy to change. Some programs change too frequently. We know of one manager that had a new program every month giving employees and customers whiplash.

There is tendency prevalent in business and in church ministry to see what other successful organizations are doing and copy their programs. This can be deadly to an organization because the copier may not have the same values and priorities.

Merely changing or starting new programs is not the answer to success.

John Wimber was a well-respected church growth expert before he started the church that became the center of the Vineyard movement in the 1980's. His church in Anaheim grew to over five thousand in attendance each Sunday. Because of his success, other churches began to copy his programs - contemporary music, small groups meeting in homes, informal dress code, and emphasis on being naturally supernatural. As other churches copied some of the programs few became as successful. The problem was they did the programs but they did not have the values and priorities of Wimber. He had a heart for the lost and his priority was not to grow a big church, but to make it easier, and provide opportunities, for an outsider to experience God. These values and priorities led to the Vineyard's practices, personnel, and programs

Managers are often prone to looking around to see what other successful organizations are doing and trying to copy their programs without understanding what the programs are designed to accomplish. Form needs to follow function.

The Japanese auto makers. In the 1960's, started a program of "quality circles." The result was a more reliable product. When American automakers copied the "quality circles" it did not work as well, in fact it slowed down production. What the Americans missed was that the function of the circles was to get input from the workers giving them ownership of the manufacturing process. In America the workers talked about what was wrong with the processes and but never felt any ownership. As a result the conversion to Total Quality Management was a slow process.

Chapter 4 - Chemistry

Bringing together often diverse elements to form a homogeneous organization can be a difficult task resembling the science of chemistry. There are differences in personality types, leadership styles, and innate capability. We find introverts and extroverts, leaders and followers, long and short range thinkers who all must work together for the success of the organization.

> *In everyday interactions introverts may avoid highly stimulating settings because they realize, perhaps only tacitly, that their performance is often compromised in such environments. When observed doing this they may be misconstrued as being antisocial. Conversely, extroverts seek out arousing settings precisely because they have learned that they perform better when engaged in the cut and thrust of animated, even heated exchanges.[26]*

> *Traditional concepts of successful people focused on the Introvert/extrovert, but more recent personality data*

---

[26] Little, Brian R (2014-10-14). Me, Myself, and Us: The Science of Personality and the Art of Well-Being (p. 38). Public Affairs. Kindle Edition.

Building to Last
demonstrates that introverts can be just as powerful and successful as extroverts.[27]

Personality type theories describe typical patterns of awareness resulting from world view and opinion. Organizations themselves can be described in terms of Type theory. There is a critical difference between a natural science and a social discipline. The physical universe displays natural laws that describe objective reality. Natural laws are constrained by what can be observed. These laws are stable and tend to change slowly over time.

> *"A natural science deals with the behavior of objects. But a social discipline such as management deals with the behavior of people and human institutions. The social universe has no 'natural laws' of this kind. It is thus subject to continuous change; and this means that assumptions that were valid yesterday can become invalid and, indeed, totally misleading in no time at all.[28]*

Peter F. Drucker, in his recent book, <u>Management Challenges for the 21st Century</u>, discusses seven major assumptions, by experts in the field of management for most of the 20th century, which are now obsolete. He then provides eight new assumptions for the 21st century. Drucker emphasizes that organizations cannot succeed by maintaining the old assumptions.[29]

Three Old Assumptions for the Discipline of Management

- Management is Business Management

---

[27] Little, Brian R (2014-10-14). Me, Myself, and Us: The Science of Personality and the Art of Well-Being (p. 1). Public Affairs. Kindle Edition.

[28] Peter F. Drucker, Management Challenges for the 21st Century, Harper Business, 1999 pp 1-2

[29] Peter F. Drucker, Management Challenges for the 21st Century, Harper Business, 1999

- There is one right organization structure.

- There is one right way to manage people.

Four Old Assumptions for the <u>Practice</u> of Management

- Technologies, markets and end-users are given.

- Management's scope is legally defined.

- Management is internally focused.

- The economy as defined by national boundaries is the "ecology" of enterprise and management.

According to Drucker, most of these assumptions were valid until the early 1980's but now they are out dated.

"They are now so far removed from actual reality that they are becoming obstacles to the Theory and even more serious obstacles to the Practice of Management. Indeed, reality is fast becoming the very opposite of what these assumptions claim it to be." [30]

Drucker's new assumptions for the social discipline of management have been slightly edited here for brevity.

Management is the specific and distinguishing organ of any and all organizations. There is not one right organizational structure. There is not one right way to manage people. One does not "manage" people. The task is to lead people. And the goal is to make productive the specific strengths and knowledge of each individual.

Technologies and End-Users are not fixed and given. Increasingly, neither technology nor end-use is a foundation of management policy. They are limitations. The foundations have to be customer values and customer decisions on the distribution of their disposable income. It is with those that management policy and management strategy increasingly will have to start.

---

[30] Peter F. Drucker, ibid

Management's scope is not only legally defined. The new assumption on which management, both as a discipline and as a practice, will increasingly have to base itself is that the scope of management is not just legal. It has to be operational. It has to embrace the entire process. It has to be focused on results and performance across the entire economic chain.

Management's scope is not politically defined. National boundaries are important primarily as restraints. The practice of management - and by no means for business only - will increasingly have to be defined operationally rather than politically.

The Inside is not the only Management domain. The results of any institution exist only on the outside.

Management's concern and management's responsibility are everything that affects the performance of the institution and its results - whether inside or outside, whether under the institution's control or totally beyond it.

Conflict Resolution

When was the last time you lost sleep over an issue? What was that issue about? Often it was concern over a relationship or conflict in a relationship. Psychologist Les Parrot[31] describes what he calls "High maintenance relationships." You will find these people in every organization and you must watch your step around them.

- The Critic: Constantly complains and gives unwanted advice.

- The Martyr: Forever the victim and wracked with self-Pity.

- Wet Blanket: Pessimistic and automatically negative.

- The Steam Roller: Blindly insensitive to others.

- The Gossip: Spreads rumors and leaks secrets.

- The Control Freak: Unable to let go and let be.

- The Back Stabber: Irrepressibly two faced.

- The Cold Shoulder: Disengages and avoids contact.

- The Green Eyed Monster: Seethes with envy.

- The Volcano: Builds up steam and is ready to erupt.

- The Sponge: Constantly in need and gives nothing back.

- The Competitor: Keeps score. Keeps track of tit for tat.

---

[31] Parrott, Les, High Maintenance Relationships How to Handle Impossible People, Tyndale House, 1996

- The Work Horse: Always pushes and is never satisfied.

- The Flirt: Imparts innuendos, which may border on harassment.

- The Chameleon: Eager to please and avoids conflict.

In all organizations there will be conflict. Conflict is unavoidable. If there is a relationship that does not have any conflict from time to time then one side has become a doormat. This leads to dysfunction in the relationship.

When there is no conflict in an organization, you can usually bet that the organization is not moving. Conflict is a result of friction. Friction is the force resisting the relative motion of surfaces, layers, and elements sliding against each other. Friction is the counterforce to movement. When there is movement, there will be friction opposing that movement.

Causes of Conflict

- Human nature. It is human nature to be competitive and argumentative.

- Divisive people: No matter where they are, some people just thrive on discord and sow it where ever they go.

- Hurting People. Hurting people hurt people. When people are hurting inside they tend to strike out and hurt others.
  The first thing to ask when someone causes conflict is, "Is that a hurting person?"

- Political People. Controlling people usually cause conflict.

- Poor Leadership. Sometimes the leaders cause conflict, and many times add to it. They may want to just keep the pot stirred

There are seven steps to resolving conflict in the workplace.

1. **Look At Yourself**. Coping with difficult people is always a problem especially if the difficult person is you. If one person tells you that you are wrong, you may ignore it. But if several people tell you that you are wrong, it might be time to listen.

2. **Look at the other person.** Try to see things from his or her perspective

3. **Meet together as soon as possible.** Do not just ignore the problem. When conflict arises we are tempted to procrastinate or rationalize that there really is no problem.

4. **Outline the issue.** Describe what you perceive that the other person is doing to cause the issue. Tell how this makes you feel. Tell why this is important to you. Ask what we are going to do about resolving the issue.

5. **Encourage a response.** The people affected are going to feel shock, bitterness and resentment. And they may not spare your feelings.
   Whatever they say or keep to themselves- they won't be ready to listen to the reason this is happening to them until they have expressed their emotions or had time to swallow their hurt. When confronting a person about a problem I have found that 50 % do not realize there is a problem, 30%Realize there is a problem but don't know how to solve it. 20% realize there is a problem but don't want to solve it. It should be noted that 80% of the time there is potential to solve the problem

6. **Speak the truth with Love and Gentleness.** Unsolvable conflict is almost always because of a

wrong attitude, not because of the issue. There will be three types of people; hiders who won't share the truth, hurlers who share the truth like throwing a hand grenade into the room, and healers that share the truth in love

7. **Write down the action to be taken.** Place the focus on the future. The action plan should include:

- The Issue

- An agreement to solve the issue

- Concrete ways that demonstrate the issue has been solved.

- An accountability structure to deal with the issue.

- A Time frame to revisit the issue.

- A commitment by both sides to put the issue in the past once it is solved.

Confrontation is necessary for the resolution of conflict and there are certain goals that confrontation is intended to achieve better understanding, positive change, and growing relationship.

When I am getting ready to reason with a man, I spend one-third of my time thinking about myself and what I am going to say - and two-thirds thinking about him and what he is going to say. [Abraham Lincoln]

When confronting a person about a problem studies have shown that; Fifty percent don't even realize there is a problem, thirty percent realize there is a problem but don't know how to solve it, twenty percent realize there is a problem but don't want to solve it, and eighty percent of the time there is the potential to resolve the problem.

Unresolved conflict is almost always because of a wrong attitude and is not because of the issue. In a conflict, there are three types of people; Hiders who do not share the truth, Hurlers who launch a weapon in your direction, they share the truth but not in Love, and healers who share the truth in love

Place the focus on the future, not the past problems. Develop and action plan. The action plan should include:

- The Issue

- An agreement to solve the issue

- Concrete ways that demonstrate the issue has been resolved.

- Include an accountability structure to deal with the issue.

- A Time frame to revisit the issue.

- A commitment by both sides to put the issue in the past once it is solved.

In order to resolve conflict, it is mandatory that there be a confrontation. But confronting conflict is difficult. We are afraid that we will be disliked, misunderstood, or rejected. We may be concerned that confrontation will make things worse. We do not know how the other person will react. For some it is not easy to share feelings. And most important many do not have the skills required to confront another.

How we handle conflict in our lives, in our business and in our organizations will go a long way in determining our success.

There are several wrong ways to handle conflict.

- The "Winner Take All" approach.

The winner take all approach is based upon the concept that one side is completely right and the other side is completely wrong. There is no in between and no room for compromise. This approach leads to hard feelings on both sides and results in gridlock. A good example can be seen in Washington DC and other governments around the world.

- The "Peace at Any Price" approach.

The opposite of "Winner Take All" is the "Peace at any Price" reaction to conflict. This is a dysfunctional reaction that leads to bullying and will preclude productive discussions.

- The "Ignore the Significance" approach. This is the "Hear no evil/ see no evil" approach. We say, "It's no big deal."

This reaction to conflict is close to the "Peace at any Price" category. The difference is that one or both sides claim that the argument is not important. This may be true at times but could lead to missing an opportunity for change that could enhance the operation of the organization.

Wade around it, the "Tiptoe Through the Tulips" approach.

If we ignore the problem, it may go away, but what really happens when the conflict is ignored is it begins to boil up inside and eventually explodes.

- The "Keeping Score" approach. "It is my turn."

There are people that Wharton professor Adam Grant calls "Matchers." Matchers will never give something away unless they get something in return. They act the same way when conflict arises. They may say, "You had your way last time. Now it's my time to win."

- The "Positional" approach. Using rank, age or prestige to impose one's will.

This is more obvious but also more disturbing when the higher up claims victory because he is more important.

You can manage conflict constructively or destructively.

Constructive	Destructive
Agree on a time and place to talk it out	Catch the other person off guard
Assertively, honestly express your feelings	passively suppress your feelings
Depersonalize. Focus on the problem, not on the person	Personalize the disagreement- "She's never liked me."
Select a neutral referee	Get your friends to referee
Develop a positive mature attitude	Be negative and as vindictive as possible
When something goes wrong, search for a solution.	When something goes wrong, find someone to blame.
Focus on specifics and simplify the situation.	Generalize and exaggerate what you consider to be the other person's wrongs.
Be open and available	Be silent and superior
When problems arise, work them out.	When problems arise , walk out
Listen, wait and learn	Presume, assume and dominate
Forgive and forget	Stubbornly demand guarantees.

There are several stages in the conflict process which are important to recognize. It starts with some kind of conflict or hurt. Then if it is not quickly resolved there will be a downward spiral where the conflict becomes harder to resolve. When the conflict is not resolved at the first stage it will degenerate to the next stage. If not resolved at that point it will continue downward.

Remedy Stage

At this stage there is a desire to fix the problem. At this point there is recognition that a problem exists, but a disagreement as to how it should be settled. There is a commitment by both sides to resolve the problem and a belief that it can be solved. Communications between the sides is honest.

If the problem is not solved it moves to the repositioning stage.

Repositioning Stage

The focus is no longer on solving the problem; it shifts to protecting one's self. People are nervous, they begin to generalize, and lose trust in the other side. Communications now becomes guarded.

If the problem is not solved it moves to the rights stage.

Rights Stage

People declare their rights. "I'm right so you must be wrong." Others join in the conflict and pick sides. They begin to assign labels to the opposition. Resolving the problem shifts from finding a solution to winning. Additional people are brought in to the conflict in the hopes that one side will outnumber the other proving the truth of their position. Communications becomes overstated and distorted.

If the problem is not solved it moves to the removal stage.

Removal Stage

"We have got to get rid of those people." The sides are no longer satisfied with getting their own way, now they want to eliminate those who they oppose. The goal at this stage is divorce. People have divided into different camps with a clear leader in each. Trust is gone.

If the problem is not solved it moves to the revenge stage.

Revenge Stage

"Someone is going to pay." People are not satisfied with separation and resignation, they seek revenge. They become fanatics and feel it is immoral to stop fighting. The conflict has become very personal and goes out of bounds.

The Superior Performer

Do you really want to hire superior performers? This may seem like a strange question, but there are certain issues that must be considered.

> *These cases illustrate the fact that, in most hierarchies, super-competence is more objectionable than incompetence. Ordinary incompetence, as we have seen, is no cause for dismissal: it is simply a bar to promotion. Super-competence often leads to dismissal, because it disrupts the hierarchy, and thereby violates the first commandment of hierarchal life: the hierarchy must be preserved*[32] *[From the Peter Principle by Laurence J. Peter]*

Jack walked into the basement laboratory of a major telecommunications company at two AM on a Saturday morning. He was an imposing figure at six feet tall, well over three hundred pounds, and dressed in a tuxedo. It was Chicago in the late sixties, and we were testing an electronic switchboard for compliance to military security requirements. Jack was the project manager of the systems which had just failed their compliance tests. That was the initial meeting of what became a long and interesting relationship. Over the next several months we became friends as we worked together to resolve the issues with his project. He became a good friend professionally, but Jack led a strange life. He was brilliant person but often a disruptive influence in meetings. We had not seen each other for about ten years. I learned that Jack was now living in New Jersey, still employed by the same firm, and now held a substantial leadership position. I wondered about his success because of his often coarse behavior and total lack of political correctness. Visiting him on my next trip to his area,

---

[32]   Peter, Laurence J.; Hull, Raymond (2014-04-01). The Peter Principle: Why Things Always Go Wrong (p. 34). HarperCollins. Kindle Edition.

I wondered if he had changed. When we met I realized he had not changed.

Still overweight, he grabbed me in a bear hug so strong I lost my breath. Then he broke out in laughter, "I got to tell you what happened the other night. I was in a saloon and a fight started. As I was swinging away, this guy comes down the stairway behind me and was ready to jump me. I saw him as I turned and swung and hit him right on the jaw. And guess what? I knocked him right out of his shoes. His shoes were still on the stairs when he landed against the wall."

After quick lunch in the company's executive cafeteria we walked back to Jack's massive office. As he sat down, tears came into his eyes as explained that he had recently lived out one of his lifelong dreams. He had been invited to play classical guitar at the iconic Carnegie Hall in New York City. In addition to being a bar room brawler and electronics company executive, Jack was an accomplished classical musician. He invited me to come back the next day and he would introduce me to some people that could help us introduce our products into some of their newer projects. That Jack did not show up the next day. Instead, his secretary informed me that Jack had worked all night and left pages of instructions for her. One of the instructions was an itinerary for me to meet six different engineering managers to evaluate how we might be mutually beneficial. What an interesting person.

Jack is what is known by organizational psychologists as a "Superior Performer." We are all familiar with the eighty-twenty rule. In business or any organization eighty percent of the work is accomplished by twenty percent of the workers. Everyone knows by experience, and objective studies have confirmed, that there are great differences in the effectiveness between workers with the same apparent skills and abilities. Some are capable but not exceptional people who simply work very hard. There are others in the twenty percent categories that are "Superior Performers." This defined Jack to a tee.

Superior performers have the energy and personal resources needed to take on demanding responsibilities. Their capabilities are likely to exceed the demands of almost any job. Sometimes they are referred to as "Young Turks" because they are frequently controversial and seem prone to trouble. This kind of person needs direct challenges rather than security. They need heavy responsibility rather than support and guidance. The superior performer is not superhuman and not as rare as one might imagine. Almost every organization of any size will already have a few superior, or potentially superior, performers on the payroll.

The problem is that if they are not in a position where they have the freedom to utilize their resources, their capabilities are often unrecognized by management and even, surprisingly, by themselves. The superior performer may not know himself well enough to understand his capabilities. His very nature keeps him from being able to apply himself well to a job that requires less than his fullest effort. In a position where he cannot extend himself, he becomes frustrated, begins to doubt his abilities, and is very likely to appear as the least likely to mark for advancement.

As a subordinate he tends to resist authority, often fails to attend to routine details, and plays games with his job and practical jokes when he becomes bored. He would be the one that sets fire to the waste basket. His single-minded search for an interesting challenge is likely to carry him over into other people's areas of responsibility. He may be seen as being after everyone's job. Not infrequently, he stimulates hasty conferences aimed at deciding what to do with him. Admittedly, such a person may turn out to be little more than the total of his faults - a pain in the neck for everyone - but he may also prove to be almost immediately capable of top-flight performance if given the opportunity.

Organizational psychologists have found through testing and counseling this type of person that he tends to possess a fairly specific pattern of characteristics. It isn't difficult to identify someone capable of making really significant contributions to an organization. The real problem is that of channeling and controlling his talents while at the same time giving him his head. The following items are the general characteristics of the superior performer:

He is mature, in the sense of being willing and able to tackle difficult and demanding assignments and to stick with tasks which are personally unpleasant for him. In fact, he will actively push for additional responsibility. His approach to problems is constructive and solution minded. He consistently looks for ways of resolving problems, not ways of getting rid of them.

He does not see personal responsibility as a burden, and he expects to be held accountable for his performance.

He is typically a bright person who enjoys tasks which present intellectual challenge. Frequently, though not necessarily, he is highly objective and analytical in his approach to problems. But regardless of whether he relies more on analytical thinking or on intuition, his ideas, when meaningfully directed, are generally sound and workable.

He is basically an individualist. He has a mind of his own, wants to do things in his own way, and needs to draw his own conclusions and make his own decisions. Such a person is poorly suited for functioning in a tightly structured environment where he is expected to go by the book and has little opportunity to apply his own thinking to his work. He is decidedly not a yes man.

He demonstrates a superior level of conceptualizing ability in evaluating problems. He is able to integrate what others might see as unimportant or unrelated details into meaningful concepts. He is quick to grasp the fundamentals and see various eventualities in any situation. Planning for the future and taking advantage of developments as they occur are capabilities in which he excels. Such a person usually demonstrates superior abilities in organizational planning as well.

He works well under pressure. In fact, he is essentially incapable of operating at his best unless he is sufficiently challenged.

Intellectually challenging games have a fascination for him. These are the sorts of games which require planning, strategy, and conceptualizing. As long as his career is adequately challenging and demanding, such games serve as an innocuous and useful outlet for excess energy; however, in the absence of sufficient career challenge, his interest in game-playing may become overblown and applied out of perspective - often without his realizing how this must appear to others. This can get him into trouble and, more than any other factor, is the reason he may come to look like the worst possible choice for advancement.

He is difficult to control. While he may be capable of conceiving and planning an entire program and then directing its implementation at every step along the way, he is equally capable of overstepping the bounds of his authority and becoming involved in areas which are none of his business. He pushes hard for his objectives, and sometimes he will forge ahead on his own initiative in the absence of specific authority to do so, taking the chance that approval will be given after the fact. It is easier for him to get forgiveness than to get permission.

He is not especially concerned about job security. He finds his security not in his position but in his capacity to perform and to achieve. His motivation leads him to rock the boat continually by introducing new concepts and procedures, and therefore he will be seen as a real threat by those who are security-minded.

Any organization which is genuinely interested in securing and utilizing people of the caliber described above has considerably more than a recruiting problem to deal with.

Chapter 5 - Leadership

Is there such a thing as a born leader? Babies are born with physical characteristics, innate intelligence, and personality which, at times, may contribute to leadership capabilities. But appearance, intelligence, and personality do not make a great leader. We inherit genes from our parents who may influence hair and eye color, intelligence, personality traits, and physical attributes. Physical attributes may influence the way we appear to others and may be a factor in their perception of our leadership qualifications.

Early in my career I was asked to write a series of articles for a trade journal. Sometime later, while attending an industry conference, I met for the first time two of the vice presidents of a major competitor. They both were well over six feet tall and towered over my average height. They looked as if they had played college football or basketball. They had read my series of articles and had been impressed. But, their very first comment after we were introduced was very telling about some people's perception of leaders, "You are much smaller than we had imagined." History has shown that presidential elections are most often won by the taller of the candidates. There is some correlation between size and popularity, but it does not necessarily reflect in leadership ability. Unfortunately the success of tall presidents has not always been reflected in successful leadership. Strong physical attributes may give the appearance of leadership potential but numerous studies reveal that size is not important when it comes to the quality of a leader.

In ancient Israel the people demanded a king. So Samuel the prophet, at God's direction, anointed Saul as king. Saul was the consummate figure of a king – tall, handsome, and charismatic. But Saul was later rejected because of his leadership and moral failures. At God's direction, the prophet Samuel was sent to the small town of Bethlehem to anoint a new king for Israel from the sons of Jesse. There were eight sons, but only seven were invited to meet with Samuel. All were strong physical specimens. As each son came forward, Samuel was impressed, but the Lord said, "No." Samuel had to ask if there were any more sons. There was one more, of whom the Bible describes as "The least of the brothers." He was out in the fields tending the sheep. That brother, David, the youngest, and the least, was selected by God and anointed by Samuel to become the next king over Israel to replace Saul. Under David's rule the state of Israel grew to the pinnacle of power and influence in the Middle East.

You cannot pick a leader by appearance, but by the number of people following behind. If you want to know whether you are a leader, look behind you, if there are people following, you are leading. You can learn all about leadership, you can think you are a good leader, but the proof is in who is following you. Leaders lead and there will be people who follow. Followers imitate the leader. In the same way, the people following you will act and do many of the same things you do. If you are generous with your resources they will copy you. If you are doing great things and no one is with you, you are probably not leading them. The bottom line is this; if you are a leader, with people following, and you want those people to change, then you will first have to change yourself.

If you find that people are not following you, it is not their fault. You must learn to be a leader and work to improve your leadership skills. So what makes a leader? Popular author and leadership guru, John C. Maxwell,[33] often notes that, "Leadership is influence." If Maxwell is correct, to become a better leader you must gain more influence. Organizational psychologist, Adam Grant, in his recent book *"Give and Take, A Revolutionary Approach to Success"* suggests there are two ways to gain influence:

---

[33] www.johnmaxwell.com

Research suggests that there are two fundamental paths to influence: dominance and prestige. When we establish dominance, we gain influence because others see us as strong, powerful, and authoritative. When we earn prestige, we become influential because others respect and admire us.[34]

Grant lists three types of individuals in the work place; givers, takers, and matchers. Takers are the ones who try to get all they can from others. They will take advantage of fellow workers to ensure their position and never give anything in return. They will often resort to dominance to get their way and satisfy their desires. Givers seek to help others grow and be successful. Unfortunately takers and others often take advantage of the givers while givers may help others to the detriment of their own work. As a result givers are often overlooked for promotion. The third category, Grant explains, are matchers. Matchers want to trade. They feel the need to reciprocate. They keep score, and will often give something in order to get something in return.

According to Grant, those who would dominate will raise their voices, promote their accomplishments, and use powerful body language. While dominance may have an immediate impact on people, it is usually short lived. Domination is something we are all familiar with growing up. In my third grade school yard, Mrs. Kraft ruled. She made sure that everyone toed the line. But when she was gone or not watching, it was the biggest and strongest kid that was in charge. That kid ruled by domination. Dominance often moves from the school yard, to the board room, the production line, office, and sometimes the pulpit. Dominance can be either positional, "I am the boss," or powerful, "I am bigger than you." Dominance is not always bullying, but it can end up there.

---

[34] Grant Ph.D., Adam M. (2013-04-09). Give and Take: A Revolutionary Approach to Success (p. 130). Penguin Group US.

In contrast those who gain influence through prestige communicate less powerfully and often show vulnerability. Prestige is gained through the leader's character, identity, purpose, integrity, and helpfulness. Prestige is a much more civilized approach to influence. Prestige is developed by consistently modeling integrity, self-identity, purpose, and a concern for those you lead.

Grant continues by identifying two types of givers. There is the "selfless" giver who is often taken advantage of by others. He is a super candidate for early burn out. He will also have a difficult time completing his own work because he is helping others accomplish their work. As a result may often be passed over for promotion. The second type of giver is the "other-ish" giver. The other-ish giver thrives while helping others to achieve their goals while still working effectively. Grant demonstrates that the "other-ish" giver will ultimately be more successful in leading an organization than the "takers" or "matchers" who have similar positions. The "other-ish" givers consider their own time and efforts important, but are always willing to help others. The figure below demonstrates this principle. Your greatest success id found when you place yourself somewhere in the upper right quadrant.

	Concern for others interests →	
Selfish Takers	Otherish Successful Givers
Apathetic	Selfless Self-Sacrificing Givers

(left axis label: Concern for self Interest)

Before every commercial airliner takes off, we hear the cabin attendant make the obligatory oxygen mask announcement. They always conclude with a statement appropriate for givers, "If you are traveling with someone that requires assistance, put your own mask on first, and then assist your fellow passenger."

If you are a giver, make sure that you take care of yourself so that you will be able to help others.

Management Versus Leadership

"Management is doing things right; Leadership is doing the right things."
[Peter Drucker]

A program review meeting was being held in a large conference room at the iconic Hotel Del Coronado in San Diego, CA just outside the gates of North Island Naval Air Station. The room was filled with senior military officers from the Army, Navy and Marine Corps. They had gathered to review the programs which shared a common technology. Each branch of the military ran their own program differently. Speaker after speaker described their particular service's approach to the problem, methodology, resources, issues, and their progress. The Army and Navy offered many presenters - civilian managers, technical experts, and uniformed military officers. The final presenter of the meeting was the lone Marine in attendance - a major with a chest full of medals. His presentation was brief, complete, and described a succession of victories over the technological problems which continued to plague his sister services. The Marine Corps budget for this project was minuscule compared with that of the other services. When the Marine major finished his presentation to the wild applause of the other attendees, the Navy Captain in charge of the meeting arose and made a comparative statement,

> *"What we have here is the difference between management and leadership. The Army and Navy are managing their programs, and have made some progress. The Marines, on the other hand have been demonstrating leadership and are way ahead of us in resolving the issues we all face. They have succeeded while we still struggle."*

Organizational consultant and author, Warren Bennis,[35] widely regarded as a pioneer of the contemporary field of leadership studies, lists twelve characteristics which distinguishes a leader from a manager.

The leader innovates.	The manager administers
The leader is an original.	The manager is a copy;
The leader develops.	The manager maintains;–
The leader focuses on people.	The manager focuses on systems and structure–
The leader inspires trust.	The manager relies on control;
The leader has a long-range perspective.	The manager has a short-range view;
The leader asks what and why.	The manager asks how and when;
The leader's eye is on the horizon.	The manager has his or her eye always on the bottom line;

---

[35] Bennis, Warren, On Becoming a Leader, Basic Books; Fourth Edition, Fourth Edition (March 3, 2009)

The leader originates.	The manager imitates
The leader challenges.	The manager accepts the status quo;
The leader is his or her own person.	The manager is the classic good soldier;
The leader does the right thing.	The manager does things right;

Values of a Leader

In his August 20, 2014 Blog Post, Wharton professor and author Adam Grant quoted Malcolm Gladwell's bold prediction.

Fifty years from now, Apple will still be around and Microsoft will be gone, but Bill Gates will be remembered — and Steve Jobs won't.

Gladwell was speaking at the Toronto Public Library's Appel Salon, and had some interesting insights about entrepreneurs in our culture.

"Gates is the most ruthless capitalist, and then he wakes up one morning and he says, 'enough.' And he steps down, he takes his money, he takes it off the table.

"I firmly believe that 50 years from now, he will be remembered for his charitable work, no one will even remember what Microsoft is."

"And of the great entrepreneurs of this era people will have forgotten Steve Jobs. Who's Steve Jobs again? There will be statues of Gates across the third world."

The greatest entrepreneurs are amoral. It's not that they're immoral, it's that they're amoral," ......

"They are completely single-minded and obsessively focused on the health of their enterprise," said Gladwell. "That's what makes them good at building businesses, but that's what also makes them people who are not worthy of this level of hagiography."

Building to Last
"So we need to be clear when we venerate entrepreneurs what we are venerating," said Gladwell. "They are not moral leaders. If they were moral leaders they wouldn't be great businessmen. So when a businessman is a great moral leader, it is because they have maintained their conscience separately from their operations."

At the very core of who we are is our values; "What is most important to us?" Earlier we discussed organizational core values which reflected the values of the founder or leader. But leadership itself has values which may vary from those of the organization. Leaders lead, they guide and facilitate the growth of others and the fulfillment of the mission of the organization. Values set priorities which result in practices which show up in programs.

Leadership values inform function. An understanding of what people believe and value will reveal their potential for success. The leader's core values will determine how he will lead and how successful he will be over the long run. Good leaders are visionary, they value integrity, and they have a concern for others.

George Mason University in Fairfax, Virginia provides a list their core leadership values.[36]

Respect: As demonstrated by self-respect and respecting others regardless of differences; treating others with dignity, empathy and compassion; and the ability to earn the respect of others.

Making a Difference: as demonstrated by personal efforts that lead to making a positive impact on individuals, systems, and/or organizations or positively affecting outcomes.

---

[36] http://masonleads.gmu.edu/about-us/core-leadership-values/

Integrity: as demonstrated by moral courage, ethical strength, and trustworthiness; keeping promises and fulfilling expectations.

Authenticity: as demonstrated by consistency, congruency, and transparency in values, beliefs, and actions; integrating values and principles to create a purposeful life and to contribute to the growth of others.

Courage: As demonstrated by possessing strength of self to act with intention on behalf of the common good; taking a stand in the face of adversity; acting boldly in the service of inclusion and justice.

Service: As demonstrated by commitment that extends beyond one's own self-interest; personal humility for the sake of a greater cause.

Humility: As demonstrated by a sense of humbleness, dignity and an awareness of one's own limitations; open to perspectives different from one's own.

Wisdom: As demonstrated by a broad understanding of human dynamics and an ability to balance the interests of multiple stakeholders when making decisions; can take a long term perspective in decision-making.

Leaders must, above all else, value integrity. When leaders speak, they must speak the truth without exaggeration. When they make promises, they must follow through. When they speak they must be accurate. They must be honest and careful with money, both their personal finances and those of the organization. The leader must be morally sound and must live what they preach. In today's world there appears to be a lack of character and integrity in our nation and the world. This lack of integrity in our leaders screams at us daily from the news media as another politician or business executive is caught lying, stealing, or being caught in immorality.

Our list of leadership values also includes;

Vision: Leaders must be able to transcend time. They cannot just live in the present. They must understand the past, live in the present, and have clear view of the future.

Identity: The leader must know themselves – their purpose, their destiny, their abilities and limitations,

Servant-hood: The leader must realize that he is in his position to help and serve others.

Courage: The leader must have the courage to keep going when things become difficult. He must have the courage to continue to the organizations goals.

Hope: Hope encourages the leader that the goal can be achieved.

The eight year old child stood on the limb of the elm tree, eyes focused on the branch of another tree six feet away. In his mind he thought. It was spring and the leaves of both trees had come into fullness. In his youthful mind he thought, "If I jumped from this limb and caught the limb across the way, I could get to the other tree." He had seen squirrels do it a thousand times and there was no one around to laugh at him if he failed. Calculating the distance, he knew it was within his range. He had jumped twice that distance on the ground many times before. All he had to do was grab that distant branch at a point where it would be sturdy enough to hold him and not break. Poised on one branch, he focused on the branch across the way. The ground, twenty feet below, faded from his sight, the leaves around him disappeared in the mist as his field of view narrowed to the target branch six feet from his perch. He crouched, then with a mighty upward thrust of legs he flew through the air, arms outstretched to grasp the limb waiting on the other side. But he had miscalculated. He had forgotten one detail. When jumping from a tree branch, much of the forward thrust is absorbed by the flexing of the limb. His flight was path was cut precisely in half. Instead of catching the sturdy limb, he grabbed a skinny branch covered with leaves. Gravity took over as his weight was no match for the poor skinny limb. He held on tight and began to ride the branch downward. His fall was slowed by the bending and then breaking of the branch but he still held on. When the branch broke he plummeted to the ground still holding tightly to the now free limb. The ground stopped the fall abruptly as his coccyx bone cracked.

Life itself is full of risks. There are some people that want to control our lives so there will be no risk. They would pass laws on children climbing trees. Imposition of rules and regulations are attempts to take the risk out of driving, flying, and even eating and smoking.

Courage begins with fighting battles over our own character, self-discipline and will.

"The first and best victory is to conquer self." [Plato]

"We have found the enemy, and it is us." [Pogo]

Our biggest obstacle is ourselves. Our flesh encourages us to live in our comfort zone, which is boring and without the dynamism that many desire.

Courage is a function of "Cause" and "Circumstances." When our cause is big enough to outweigh our circumstances, we are willing to risk. Just imagine the cause of being able to fly from one tree to the next like the squirrels. The eight year old boy was willing to risk falling because his cause was great. No one was watching. It was not for fame or fortune. The cause was fulfillment of a dream. The cause was the satisfaction of accomplishing something dangerous. It was akin to going over Niagara Falls in a barrel. It was Columbus sailing into the unknown, risking falling off the end of the earth. It was Sir John Franklyn setting out to find the Northwest Passage.

When the circumstances outweigh the cause, we will not take the risk. That is why our purpose/cause must be bigger than our circumstances.

It takes courage to be a leader.

Several years ago in India, we noted that there were millions of people living in shelters constructed of animal dung or under bridges and viaducts. In addition in the city of Mumbai there are over a million homeless people. Each morning we watched trucks come around to pick up the corpses of those who had not lived through the night. India has become a progressive nation. They have legally eliminated the caste system. It is the world's largest democracy. Yet with all of the social programs in place, a large part of the population still lives without hope. Many live their lives without the hope of their situation ever getting better.

Chuck and Joan Hartzell felt God calling them away from their comfortable lives in the Seattle suburb of Kirkland, Washington to something new, but as yet, they did not know what it would be. Chuck was an orthopedic assistant with the Veterans Administration and Joan was a registered physical therapist and visiting nurse. It was then they saw pictures and heard reports of the poverty, sickness, and hopelessness of people in India. Soon, Chuck and Joan headed for India to help set up a medical clinic. They sold their house and gave away most of their possessions to live in the village of Kuppadi in Kerala state on the southwest tip of India. While helping with the clinic, they saw the plight of a caste of villagers who had been potters for generations.

Their ancient pottery vocation was dying because of more efficient modern manufacturing processes. Aluminum and plastic pots had replaced clay pottery for cooking and cleaning. As a result, the pottery business was disappearing. So, too, were the hopes of these potters and their families. The Hartzells had an idea to start a small business. The potters would make their pottery and the Hartzells would sell the pottery in the United States. They did not know how to make pots, but chose to learn so they could incorporate practices that would be acceptable for the U.S. market. Clay pots can no longer be used for cooking, but there is a market for clay decorative items in gardens and patios. When enough clay pots were completed, they loaded a 20-foot shipping container and sent it by ship to Seattle and a distribution system was established in the United States.

As the people of Kuppadi began to trust them, Chuck and Joan were able to give hope to the people in this village.

It requires hope to endure the problems and issues of this world. With hope you can endure under fire - to have the ability to withstand hardship, adversity, and stress; to remain firm under difficulty, without yielding.

> *"Every person is in certain respects like all other people, like some other people, and like no other person."*

This quote was adapted from Clyde Kluckhohn and Henry A. Murray, <u>Personality in nature, Society and Culture</u>, 1953[37]

Leaders must walk in the knowledge of who they are. They cannot develop prestige when they are trying to emulate someone else. They must know who they are and their life purpose. Many of us grow up confused about our identity. But we need to realize we are here to serve a purpose.

Leaders that know their identity and purpose can walk with self-confidence. Without an identity and purpose, we fear failure so much that we are frozen in place and cannot take the next step. We must eliminate our fears of failure, and rejection. Good people will only condemn others for not trying. They will not condemn someone for trying and failing. Home run hitters in baseball strike out more often than they hit home runs. The baseball legend Babe Ruth set the record for the most home runs in a season and also the most strikeouts in a single season.

---

[37] Little, Brian R (2014-10-14). Me, Myself, and Us: The Science of Personality and the Art of Well-Being (p. 1).

Ruth's record for strikeouts was broken by Sammy Sosa who also broke Ruth's home run record. Most people who have accomplished great things have also failed as much as they have succeeded.

Do not be afraid of what others might think. Attempt something that is worth the effort even though there will be a strong chance of failure. It is far better to attempt something great and fail than to attempt nothing and succeed.

Identity means you understand your life's purpose. Leaders must walk with purpose. We will never have peace in our lives until we understand our unique individual purpose. Our purpose will be fired by a passion which is strong enough for us to sacrifice other things in order to achieve it. Our purpose is not based entirely on the needs around us, but to satisfy a deep seated desire in our heart for self-actualization.

There is so much need in the world today that most of us fall into one of two possible groupings; those who try to do everything and those who see the task as being too huge so they give up before they start. The former category leads to early burn out while the latter group sits back and does nothing. We must find out what our particular piece of the task is and do that.

Management guru Peter Drucker[38] in his book "Management Challenges for the 21st Century" discusses five demands on modern workers. They have to ask: Who Am I? What are my strengths? How Do I work?

- They have to ask: Where do I belong?

- They have to ask: What is my contribution?

- They have to take Relationship Responsibility.

---

[38] Peter F. Drucker, Management Challenges for the 21st Century, Harper Business, 1999.

- They have to plan for the Second Half of their Lives.

These demands are paramount for leadership. With the rise of the knowledge worker, "one does not 'manage' people," Mr. Drucker wrote. "The task is to lead people. And the goal is to make productive the specific strengths and knowledge of every individual."

The conference room was filled with leaders from different parts of the organization who had come together to discuss the organization's future. This international organization had been in existence for a little over twenty years and had grown rapidly and had reached the "maximum efficiency" phase of its life cycle. Now it was facing a crisis. Two years ago, the founder had died leaving a leadership gap. His hand-picked successor carried on but now lethargy was moving into while it fell into institutionalism. The vision was lost. Different branches had gone in different directions Individual leaders had their own ideas of direction and purpose. The corporate vision had died with the founder. The purpose of this meeting was to reformulate and recast the vision. They realized that it would not be an easy task and would take several years to complete. After several days of discussions it was determined that the first issue to be addressed would be to resolve the questions of values, identity, and direction.

A school teacher once told her class, "Tonight it is going to be clear outside. When it gets real dark tonight, I want you to go into your back yard and count the stars." The next day kids reported their counts: The answers ranged from a high of one million down to the last kid who proudly announced that he had counted nineteen stars. After the shock of such a low count was over, the boy explained, "We have a very small back yard."

The Continental Congress of the thirteen American colonies met on the fourth day of July in 1776 to announce that they regarded themselves as independent states and were no longer a part of the British Empire. That day, far away in Great Britain, the king of England, George III, wrote in his diary, "Nothing important happened today."

Good leaders are visionaries. They dream big dreams. They have a vision for the future of their organization, but if there is no action the vision will remain but a dream and nothing will be realized. The visionary leader must then be able to cast the vision in a way that will motivate team members to follow his/her lead. The transformation of an organization requires the visionary to be able to turn the vision into action and excite those around him to follow.

According to author and leadership expert, John Maxwell,[39] vision requires four elements: (1) the ability to see, (2) the faith to believe, (3) the courage to do, (4) and the hope to endure.

Our ability to see is not just with the eyes. Helen Keller was once asked, "What could be worse than being blind?" She replied "Having sight, but not seeing." Vision is the ability to see beyond our limitations, beyond the size of our back yard. The "ability to see" is our awareness of what is happening in our environment. Many suffer from tunnel vision, being unable to see beyond the fences. Many are so busy doing stuff that they do not spend enough time just looking around.

Children seem to have better vision than adults because they have very vivid imaginations. Imagination is the capacity to make connections between; the seen and the unseen, the past and present, and the present and future. When imagination is healthy it allows us to think about the mysteries of our world. Vision and imagination are a team that works together. Someone once said that in our brains, the "revelator" is right next to the "imaginator."

---

[39] INJOY Life Club Volume 4, Lesson 10

A good corporate vision is one that is just over the horizon, just out of reach. So we establish visible goals that are achievable. Achievement of each goal brings us closer to our vision. Someday, that vision will be right in front of us and we can reach out and touch it.

In this fast paced world, driven by technology, we become obsessed with information and do not take time to allow our imagination to flourish. Instead we use information and explanation to manage our organizations. As a result, vision is destroyed and potential visionary leaders become managers of information and never achieve their dreams.

Organizational behaviorist, James M. Kerr lists five steps to becoming more visionary. [40]

1. Practice Re-Imagining How Things Are.

2. Adopt an Outside-In Perspective.

3. Ask "Why Not?"

4. Seek Synergies. Leverage ideas and concepts from like-minded people.

5. Integrate Disparate Ideas Into Your Thinking.

"We have always done it that way," is the death knoll to future growth. Take time to explore diverse ways of achieving the results. Two important aspects of any task are "form" and "function." Function is what we do, what we are trying to accomplish. It has to do with our vision and purpose. Form is the method we use to accomplish our function. In the game of American football, the function is twofold - to get the football across the opposing teams goal line and to keep the opponents from taking the ball across your goal line. Each team has a series of plays (forms) to use to move the ball forward. When the quarterback or coach changes the plays, it will often leads

---

[40]   http://www.inc.com/james-kerr/5-steps-to-becoming-a-visionary-leader.html

to a good gain. In a similar way, changing the form that is used in an organization to achieve its function often rejuvenates the team. When an organization has become an institution we confuse form and function and make the form the goal rather than function. The original vision often becomes dim over a long time so it cannot be restored instantaneously. It takes a significant event to make a paradigm shift and change world view. But this is required when organizational renewal is desired.

In the second century, Egyptian astronomer Ptolemy explained the universe with the earth as its center. The sun and the stars rotated around earth. Everything revolved around us. Then in the sixteenth century, Polish astronomer Copernicus proved that the earth revolves around the sun. The church called him a heretic because this new theory destroyed what their thinking had been for centuries. There was a paradigm shift. When our understanding changes, everything changes, but nothing really changes. It is only our perception of the world that has changed. The sun will still come up in the east and the sun will set in the west. Life goes on. The changes are all in our mind.

> *You don't have to sit outside in the dark; the stars do not require it. But if you want to see stars it is required. [Annie Dillard]*

"Catalyst," that was the designation given the regional leader of an international non-profit organization in the early 1990's. The board members had all taken a battery of psychological tests to determine their leadership style. The test was designed to determine the organizational chemistry of the ministry. The battery of tests categorized each leader in one of four possible styles; "entrepreneur," "catalyst," "implementer" and "maintainer." Today the terms "catalyst" or "catalytic leader" are used extensively in leadership and business literature, but in those days it was a new concept. The term catalyst in leadership is often misused and widely misunderstood. In chemistry, a catalyst is a substance added to a chemical reaction that speeds up the reaction. A catalytic leader is one who speeds up change in an organization. The opposite of a catalyst would be called an "inhibitor," one who resists change. In many organizations inhibitors exist in high places resulting in stagnation which will lead to decay.

In the late 1980's Dr. Jeff Luke of the University of Oregon conducted a research project to determine why some communities were successful in solving difficult municipal problems while others failed. His results demonstrated that problems were solved when groups, who had a stake in the issue, came together and developed a group solution. He discovered that the crucial factor for success was a specific type of leader that could bring the groups together; he named it "catalytic leadership."

> *Catalytic leadership is based on the leader engaging and motivating others to take on leadership roles, engaging everyone to work towards a common vision. [Jeff Luke]*

Authors Ori Brafman and Rod Beckstrom propose a similar conception of a catalytic leader; one who brings other leaders together to set up a decentralized organization.

> *Catalysts develop an idea, get everyone talking, lead by example, and then let the circle take on a life of its own. Once the initial spark has been provided, the catalyst then rides off into the sunset.* [41]

But a catalytic leader is more than someone that comes into the picture, brings people together and then leaves. In successful organizations there will be a mix of leadership styles. The "Entrepreneur" is the visionary that takes action to start a company or organization. Normally there will be only one entrepreneur to an organization. When there are more than

---

[41] The Starfish and the Spider - Ori Brafman and Rod Beckstrom: The Unstoppable Power of Leaderless Organizations

one, their visions may conflict. The "Catalyst" brings people together to move toward fulfilling the vision. The "implementer" is more detail oriented and will put meat on the bones of the organization and develop plans to move the vision forward. The "Maintainer" is the manager that keeps things together after the entrepreneur and catalyst have moved on to something new.

Catalytic leaders, as agents for change, communicate the vision, develop concepts, and build the organization. Many organizations today need to change or die. Change requires the presence of catalytic leadership in order to revive the vision, communicate the vision, and rebuild the organization. Unfortunately, where change is required, and it is not happening, there is probably a preponderance of "Inhibitors."

Chapter 6 - Authority

Authority is defined as: "the power or right to give orders or make decisions: the power or right to direct or control someone or something." Source of authority may be internal (residing within the leader), or external (authority vested in the leader from an external agency.)

External Authority

A policeman with a badge and uniform has the power and right to direct automobiles and trucks to stop, turn, or proceed. His authority has been vested in him by a governmental agency. His authority is identified by his badge and uniform. An impostor could steal the uniform and badge and go out in the street and direct traffic and the drivers of the vehicles would not know he was an impostor and would probably follow his direction. His authority is in his appearance. The policeman does not have the physical strength to stop a truck coming at him at a high rate of speed, but he is able to stop the truck by the authority vested in him by the government.

In a traditional business organization there is a hierarchy of authority. The Board of Directors, whose authority is vested in them by the stockholders or owners, has authority over the Chief Operating Officer, or the president. The president has authority over vice presidents. There is a hierarchal structure of authority throughout the entire organization.

Similarly a military officer gives orders to troops who are trained to be obedient and to respond quickly to proper commands. The officer's authority is vested by higher authority and backed by the government. Uniform insignia designates her rank. It shows that the officer is authority and also under authority. The military is a hierarchal organization where orders come down from the top to the lowest echelons and obedience looks up for direction.

The policeman, the company president, and the military officer have positional authority. Their power and right to give orders and control people is based upon their position within the structure. Their authority is described as "Institutional authority." It is external to the leader who exercises the power. Someone with institutional authority is normally given a title. There will be an expected behavior based upon the title one carries. Once you are given a title, it is often expected that you will be entitled to certain privileges which come with the title.

In most organizations there are people who have a title but do not exercise their authority properly. There may be a number of reasons for not exercising the positional authority that they have been given – lack of confidence, fear of retribution, or fear of failure, to name a few. They may have the title but may not be recognized by the people they are supposedly leading. Saul of ancient Israel was one with the title but not properly exercising the authority. There is a tendency with these individuals to threaten and bully others to get them to follow orders. They use domination and intimidation to get their way. They can manipulate by withholding pay, harassment, assigning difficult jobs, or providing false performance reviews. In manipulation, one person wins and another loses. There are Status symbols of external authority; uniforms, flashy dress, expensive cars, large offices, big desks, and comfortable chairs.

While visiting friends in Colorado, we stopped at a furniture store in the mountain town of Salida to visit a very special furniture store. An artisan manufactured the furniture from old tree stumps using natural wood. As we wandered through all of the rustic chairs, tables, and beds, my eyes fell on the largest, polished, wooden desk I had ever seen. The top surface of the desk was three inches thick and formed in the shape of an Australian boomerang. Its total length was a dozen feet and four foot across. It was massive and awesome. On the inside of the angle was a huge, padded leather chair matching the desk in extravagance. More of a throne than a chair, it was inviting me to sit. I had to try it out. As I sat behind the luxurious majesty of the desk I was transformed into a powerful executive, in my mind. I verbalized my first thought, "From this desk, I could rule the world!" Only slightly embarrassed, I quickly arose and moved to another room. That chair and desk shouted out, "Authority."

There is one major problem with external authority. It can be taken away quickly without any warning. As a result, external authority must be guarded and protected. When protecting your position, you will inevitably encounter someone that challenges your authority, leading to conflicts. External authority may lead to compliance from underlings, but it does not always warrant respect.

Internal Authority

Internal authority is based upon your character, the kind of person you really are. Earlier we quoted organizational psychologist and author of "Give and Take," Adam Grant, as saying that there were two ways to gain influence (have authority); dominance or prestige. Internal authority is all about "Prestige."

Internal authority may be difficult to explain but it is one of those things that "we know it when we see it."

Those with internal authority know who they are, why they are where they are, and what must be done. A person develops internal authority by growing in individuality, self-confidence, conviction, integrity, and having servant attitude.

Individuality

"To be yourself in a world that is constantly trying to make you something else is the greatest accomplishment." Ralph Waldo Emerson

Babies are born with certain characteristics inherited from their parents. They are in the inherited DNA. As they

97

grow up they learn certain behaviors that make them unique persons. If you look carefully you can see the uniqueness in each person. We often wonder how parents of identical twins can tell them apart. There are slight differences in identical twins which make each unique. To a casual observer, they are identical, but to the parent who is always close can pick up on certain characteristics that make each unique. Every individual in the world is unique. Unfortunately, because we have a desire to fit in, we try to hide our uniqueness and become like others around us. We see this in teenagers who dress alike, talk alike, and act alike. There are some who rebel and dress and act differently, but soon the rebels will come together and share their dress and actions as they fit together.

In the business world there is a tendency to dress, think, and act like colleagues in the organization. In many large corporations you see individuals who dress alike, have similar facial hair, and walk with a certain gait. Most of them are inadvertently imitating their immediate boss who in turn is copying the chief executive.

Individuality is important. It is the quality that makes one person or thing different from all others. It is not easy to be different, but you cannot develop internal authority if you are trying to be like someone else. Today we have many people in politics, business, and the church who are not sure of their own identity, so they put on masks and try to become like the ones they care about, or what they think others want them to be. They do all of this in the hope that they will be accepted.

Individuality requires an understanding of one's gifts, talents, and purpose. Purpose is derived from the call of your heart or the destiny which you want to pursue. You have to know who you are and believe that is enough. While you can grow in knowledge and ability, the only way you can grow in individuality is by being yourself and not trying to emulate someone else.

Self-confidence

Self-confidence is confidence in oneself and in one's powers and abilities. It is not prideful but it is being totally honest about who you are. You know your weakness and limitations as well as your strengths. Self-confident people have a peace about them. There is an internal strength which allows them to handle criticism and failure without reacting in self-pity and defensiveness. Self-confidence allows one to react appropriately to criticism - to be objective, analyze, and accept appropriate criticism.

Anyone who is active bringing in new ideas will be criticized. It is the nature of the game. Self-confidence allows us to look at the criticism objectively, evaluate it to determine the validity, and take action when necessary.

Conviction/purpose/focus

Individuals with internal authority have a conviction regarding what they are doing. By focusing on their purpose, they will not be sidetracked by unimportant issues which could distract and keep them from reaching their goal. Strong leaders are gifted with the ability to see long range goals and not chase down rabbit holes. Focus is derived from a conviction or purpose which evokes passion and a willingness to make sacrifices to achieve that which they seek. Passion is contagious and draws others to the battle. Others catch your passion and are led toward the same goal. People will follow leaders who have a passion about their purpose.

"I just set myself on fire and people come to watch me burn." [Johns Wesley]

Each of us has a destiny, or purpose, in life. But we often dilute our efforts by chasing after things we are not called to chase. It is better to be good at a few things than mediocre at many things.

Integrity

Integrity is measured by what you do when no one else is looking. It is the quality of being honest and fair - the state of being complete or whole. Integrity seems to be lacking in many leaders today. We are witnessing the lack of honesty and fairness by politicians, business executives, religious leaders, and individual citizens in today's world. Integrity seems to have been lost in this egocentric Post-Modern world.

"Whoever is careless with the truth in small matters cannot be trusted with important matters." [Albert Einstein]

Leaders with integrity will stand out and be followed by others seeking truth. Integrity requires us to speak the truth without exaggeration, follow through when we say we will do something, be careful in money and moral issues, live what we preach, and be a servant to those we lead - willing to sacrifice our own desires to help others.

Servant Attitude

"Not all of us can do great things. But we can do small things with great love." — Mother Teresa

A Servant attitude will always result in internal authority. A servant leader wants to benefit the group and desires to make other people successful and see them grow. It is a way of honoring others. There are too many leaders today that sacrifice the people that they have authority over, to further their own personal agenda.

Ezekiel 34:2 (MSG) "Son of man, prophesy against the shepherd-leaders of Israel. Yes, prophesy! Tell those shepherds, 'God, the Master, says: Doom to you shepherds of Israel, feeding your own mouths! Aren't shepherds supposed to feed sheep?

Increase Your Internal Authority

Internal Authority cannot be taken away. People with internal authority will always rise to the top of an organization. They do not have to be afraid of other people, they can take risks and be innovative, and they end up with external authority given to them. They will be recognized by higher authorities and do not have to rely on the external things to be successful.

Those with authority must be under authority. As an organizational leader, your selection of new leaders is important to the success of your organization. The most important question to ask before giving someone new authority is,

"Do they respond to authority in their present position?"

If they cannot be under authority, they cannot be trusted to be given more authority. If they can relate well to those over them, they will be able to relate well to those under them.

Internal authority can be increased by following the steps listed below.

Know yourself: Understand who you are; your abilities, your strengths and weaknesses, and your purpose in life.

Eliminate Fear of failure: Develop a Godly self-confidence. Baseball player, Sammy Sosa broke the record for strike outs in a single season. He hit 62 home runs breaking the record of Babe Ruth, but he struck out more often than he hit a home run. Most people who have accomplished great things have failed a couple of times. Good people only condemn others for not trying, not those who try and fail.

Eliminate Fear of Rejection: Do not be afraid of what others might think. Attempt something great. It is far better to attempt something great and fail than to attempt nothing and succeed.

Accept what you cannot change:

Be thankful:

Believe in the importance of your purpose:

Keep righteous relationships:

Don't get yourself over fatigued: When are too fatigued you fail to listen, you jump to conclusions, and you do and say things you should not do or say.

Watch your words: Leaders are more accountable. Words may have a tremendous effect on others. What you say has a big impact on others. Watch out for criticizing others behind their back. Watch promises you cannot keep. Watch saying one thing to one person and something else to another. Private conversations will not stay private. We cannot control other s but we can control our tongue.

Respect rights and emotions of others: Give them wise counsel but do not take away their ability to make their own mistakes.

Strive for excellence: A poorly written letter does not have authority.

Walk in integrity:

Walk in servant-hood:

Walk in Humility: Be honest about your weaknesses and limitations. Be a learner, don't be afraid to say, I don't know. Change your mind once in a while. Allow others to change your mind once in a while. Ask for help and advice once in a while. When you are wrong, admit it and repent quickly.

Have Faith in the future. Expect success.

Chapter 7 - Communications

Why is there such an epidemic of "poor communications" within organizations? In every one I've been in, employees have ranked it right at the top of their major issues. Indeed, [Margaret J. Wheatley][42]

Wheatley speculated that "poor communications" was just a misnomer for the real problems hidden in the organization, but she found she was wrong. Poor communications is definitely the problem in most organizations. It is not for lack of trying that management is accused of holding back. In the traditional hierarchal organization, information flows up and down the chain of command. Accuracy is often distorted between the highest levels and the lower levels. We are reminded of the game we all played as children where a message is whispered in the ear of the person next to you, then he/she would whisper to the next person and each person around the circle whispers what they heard to the next person. We were all amazed how the message changed until, in most instances, it was not even recognizable. When we are part of an organization we expect information, coming and going, to be accurate and stable. But obviously it is not.

Carol was a strong employee. Hired as an executive assistant, her job expanded rapidly because of her intelligence, strong work ethic, and hunger for challenge. But Carol had a basic personality flaw. She was a perfectionist in everything she did and expected everyone else to be a well. She had high standards for herself and also those around her. She would fly into a rage and berate others when they made a mistake or

[42] Wheatley, Margaret J. (2006-09-01). Leadership and the New Science: Discovering Order in a Chaotic World (Kindle Locations 1475-1476). Berrett-Koehler Publishers. Kindle Edition.

were sloppy in their work. In the rare times she made a mistake, it would destroy her emotionally for a time and she would have to leave to recover. Her attitude toward others came to the attention of the division director who explained to Carol's supervisor, that if she did not correct her relationships with the other staff, she would be terminated. The supervisor agreed to communicate this directly to Carol. There was a meeting and for a short time Carol seemed mellower. This lasted only a few months until she reverted back to her former attitude. This time, the director decided to take personal action with the long term and proficient employee. He called her into his office and told her, in no uncertain terms, that she had to change and if she did not change, she would be terminated.

Her response was, "I did not know it was that bad. Nobody ever told me it could cost me my job."

Obviously something was lost in the transfer of information between the General Manger, Carol's supervisor, and Carol.

This is a typical example of ineffective communications which, in a hierarchal structure, can lose something in the passing of information up and down the chain of command. The original communication between the director and Carol's supervisor was clear. But when the supervisor communicated to Carol, the urgency and importance of the message was softened. The supervisor may have been fearful of Carol's reaction or he did not want to anger his most productive employee.

Studies have shown that what we say is not half as important as how we say it. People will interpret what we are communicating in three different ways;

- fifty five percent of what they hear is based upon our facial expression and body language,

- thirty seven percent is based upon the tone of our voice,

- and only eight percent on the words that we say.

It is important in business and in our personal lives that we communicate so as to be understood.

The organization that is most effective at communicating will ultimately be the most successful.

Communications is the flow of information throughout an organization. Information is the very life blood of any organization. It can be the source of dynamic life and imbue vitality into an otherwise boring task or it can make a difficult task even more trying.

In the Newtonian management form, the supervisor is tasked is to maintain control, to keep information contained, to pass it down in such a way that no newness is imparted. In "Leadership and the New Science," Margaret Wheatley writes,

> "Information chastity belts are a central management function. The last thing we need is information running loose in our organizations."

Traditionally, the flow of information has been strictly managed with information distributed on a "need to know basis." This meant that some were purposely excluded from information. Management explained this as a need for keeping their strategies hidden from competitors fearing that rogue employees would compromise the corporation by giving away secrets. Thus Coca Cola hid its formula in a vault and only one person was privy to the combination.

The Coca-Cola Company keeps the formula for their product in a safe at their headquarters in Atlanta, Georgia. This formula is the secret recipe for Coca Cola syrup that bottlers combine with carbonated water to create its line of cola soft drinks. A high priority of the Coca-Cola Company has been to protect their product from being duplicated by their competitors. But, the food and Drug Administration (FDA) requires that manufacturers provide a clear list of ingredients on the outside of the container. In today's scientific world with its propensity for reverse engineering, nothing is safe from duplication. Any competent chemical engineer could buy a coke, analyze it, and create an exact duplicate. Still Coca Cola Company continues to fuel the image of the secret vault, with the recipe hidden inside, available to only one person. This has now become a marketing ploy.

The fact is, when management does not trust the loyalty of employees, the employees are not apt to trust management, leading to dysfunctional organizations. If information is going to be the life blood of an organization, then good communications must be a priority and the organizational structure must enable clear communications. Good communications must be a core value of every organization. It must be established in the initial startup with structure designed to encourage and facilitate the transfer of information.

We live in what author Leonard Sweet[43] describes as the TGIF era. (Twitter, Google, I-Phone, and Facebook.) Sweet marks the beginning of this age as 1973 when Martin Cooper and his team from the Motorola Corporation invented the cell phone. Sweet refers to those born after 1973 as "Googlers" while those born prior to the invention of the cell phone he refers to as "Gutenbergers." Gutenbergers grew up reading printed books. Print information was expensive to publish and distribute. Googlers on the other hand grew up with the Internet with its volume of free information.

Our world has changed, secrets are exposed, and information flows freely throughout the Internet via Google, Wikipedia, and social media. There are many branches to the Internet tree that have not yet been discovered. Anything you want to know is available somewhere - for free. In this TGIF world it is better for the business leader to be the first to reveal bad news, than to have it publicly displayed on "Face Book,"

---

[43] Sweet, Leonard, *Viral how Social Networking is Poised to Ignite Revival.* Waterbrook Press, Colorado Springs, Co 2012

"Linked In," or some other Internet source. For a strong and successful organization in the TGIF age information flow must be open and free. The management of information weakens the team approach. Information must be allowed to flow freely throughout the organization.

The mode of communications is one of the most significant organizational practices leading to success or failure. The practices used for information flow, inside and outside the organization, result from the organization's core values and priorities. The practice of communications can only be changed when we change the priorities of the organization.

Looking at court records of corporate executives, who have recently been convicted and incarcerated for fraud, shows their attempts to manage information. Most of the recent business scandals were associated with a few people controlling information about profitability in an effort to paint a more positive picture. Their motive was to convince stockholders and the market that the company was in a healthier financial condition.

It is normal for business leaders to widely disseminate good news while soft pedaling or omitting the bad news. It is a priority for some leaders and managers to look good. His reputation may be at stake. It is often a matter of pride and ego. The root of this attitude goes all the way back to a person's core values. Heads of organizations must realize that in this day and age there is no way information can be kept secret for long.

There are three things that organizational leaders must communicate regularly in order to be successful:

- Vision;

- Status - where you are today - your progress - successes and weaknesses - problems which must be overcome;

- Goals, direction and strategies for achieving the vision.

Vision is the fuel that drives an organization forward. But it is only effective when the leader can communicate his vision. In order for the vision to become the force that moves the organization, it must permeate throughout the organization. The vision must be communicated often and so clearly that employees, clients, and supporters not only know it but they must become emotionally attached. We noted earlier that words only account for eight percent of the interpretation of the message, while fifty five percent of the interpretation is derived from what is seen with the eyes. A vision must be communicated in a way that the receivers of the message can form a picture in their mind of the vision.

Most building programs are supported because they are easily envisioned. There will be drawings to look at, models set up in the lobby, bricks and mortar that can be touched There may even be an old building in disrepair which they can see needs renewal. Less tangible visions are more difficult to see and feel. They fail to motivate because of the inability to form a picture in people's minds. The may be too subtle. A vision to clean up the environment may be misunderstood but discussions of the consequences of not cleaning the environment can be described in great detail – climate change, rising oceans, polar bears losing their habitat, etc. Many worthy visions go unachieved because the leader with vision is unable to communicate that vision in a way that others can visualize.

In addition to communicating the vision itself, the benefits derived from achieving the vision must have significance. Significance will be a motivating factor for taking ownership. The vision must be big enough and have more value than the present situation. If people are satisfied where they are, doing what they have done for years, they have little reason to own the vision. Owning the vision moves the team to support the vision.

Once the vision is cast in a clear creative way, and everyone has bought in, that is not the end. That is only the beginning. There must be action. A threat to the organization will often stimulate a vision, but it can get lost in the business of every day events that may take priority over an envisioned goal.

In July 1962, The United States was testing the effects of high altitude weapons detonated in space in the middle of the Pacific Ocean. The effects were unexpected. In Hawaii, nearly nine hundred miles away three hundred street lights were knocked out, numerous burglar alarms were set off, and a microwave link was damaged.

During the sixties scientists determined the cause to be Electromagnetic Pulse. (EMP) Our civilian and military leaders envisioned hardening all the nation's strategic assets to survive the effects of EMP. Throughout the "Cold War " years the government spent billions hardening power distribution systems, major weapons systems, and communications facilities. Money was no object and everything that needed hardening was scheduled for upgrading. When the Cold War ended, the threat was reduced, the money for EMP hardening dried up, and most hardening efforts ceased. Then came the threat of terrorists or rogue nations with nuclear weapons and the power grid and communications facilities were still vulnerable. EMP hardening suddenly became a priority again.

The vision of neutralizing the EMP threat becomes lost, and now it is being reemphasized as recent movies, books, and TV shows have dramatized its effects.

Good leaders communicate, clearly, fully and regularly because people lose sight of the vision and purpose. It may only take thirty days for some to lose sight of their purpose. In the fifth century BCE, Nehemiah, a servant to the king of

109

Persia, had a vision to rebuild the wall around the city of Jerusalem. The king encouraged him to go to Israel and accomplish his vision. When he arrived he inspected the problem and saw what had to be done. He then shared the vision with the Israelites who were motivated to accomplish Nehemiah's vision. But, thirty days later, they had forgotten the vision and began to complain and fight amongst themselves. Nehemiah had to recast the vision quickly to save the project.

Many organizational vision statements are so ambiguous or so far reaching that the vision may never be achieved. A good vision statement is one that creates a picture in the mind of the reader that demonstrates a worthy cause that is measurable and progress can be charted.

Since the organizational vision is the fuel that empowers the vehicle towards a better future, it is important to keep everyone advised to the progress being made – good and bad.

When people buy into a vision, they want to understand the progress the organization is making toward achieving that vision. Regular status reports provide information on the organization at critical points in time. They can explain how you got to that point – successes and failures. They will describe problems encountered, how those problems were solved or addressed, and what problems are anticipated in the future. When the picture looks too rosy, it is time to be concerned. If an organization is progressing toward its destiny there will be problems encountered. Foreseeing potential issues is not thinking negatively it is being realistic and preparing for complications. In that way nobody will be taken by surprise.

The status report should cover all aspects of the organizations progress including financial information.

Public Corporations are required to file financial data on a regular basis to the Securities Exchange Commission, in order for there to be a fair evaluation of the stock prices. These financial statements are distributed widely to all who might invest in the corporation. Privately held corporations are not required by law to provide this information unless the state of registration requires.

Both public and private businesses are required to file income tax returns and pay their taxes to the government. In the United States, certain non-profit organizations are tax exempt and are not required by law to file income tax returns.

Two non-profit organizations had an identical problem. The first had a large budget while the second had a budget of less than one third of the first. One was in a large city the other a small town. Both were providing similar services to their respective communities. They were both supported by donations from constituents and grants from foundations. The income of both had dropped dangerously low threatening the need to reduce some services to the communities they served.

The leaders of the organizations both complained to anyone that would listen, that their income was getting lower and more cuts would be forthcoming. But the situation did not change. They were hesitant to give out the news to members, clients, and supporters in fear that they would judge their ability to lead. So the situation kept getting worse as the organization's services continued to fall. As they watched the decline they still did not want anyone to know the true status. However, it was obvious to everyone, inside and outside as their presence in the community was reduced. Eventually the leaders of both organizations decided it was time to communicate their problems to people inside the organizations and outside. Written communications were sent to every constituent, supporter, and client laying out the situation and requesting additional support.

The letter worked, people responded with the comment, "We did not know it was that bad or we would have given more."

111

This resolved both financial situations.

The third item that needs to be communicated regularly is current goals. The vision and mission statements provide an overall direction for the organization. They are their reason for existence. Goals are the means of achieving the mission/vision in bite-size steps.

Goals change regularly. As one goal is achieved, a new goal takes its place. Goals are more hard and fast. They are to be specific, definitive, achievable and measurable. In setting goals, consider the vision or mission statement of the organization, break that down into segments or legs of a journey, and then decide how and when you will get to the next leg or segment. This becomes an immediate goal. This information needs to be communicated in a way that everyone understands their role in meeting the goal.

Assume your organization wants to build a new building. The first goal would be to determine the cost of the building. Do you remodel the old building? Do you build a new one from scratch? Or do you buy an existing building? Once that decision is made, it is time to raise finances to achieve that goal. Communicating the financial goal and the progress to the goal can be communicated readily for all to see how we are going to get to the next goal as we move toward achieving our vision. As progress moves ahead or stalls there may be changes in how we move forward.

In this "Googler" age we have so many means and methods of communications which were not available to us in the past. Just fifteen years ago, our choices were written letter (snail mail), telephone, and email. Mass communications through the Post Office was costly but still reaches the Gutenbergers. Organizations and communities have set up "Robo-calling" which allows them to contact everyone to warn of dangerous activities such as an approaching hurricane or tornado.

Organizations can publish information on social media when the people who need the information are subscribing to the media and take time to check their pages. Websites and text messaging are also available. There is no lack of methods to communicate electronically to customers, employees, and friends. But still many people will never get the word.

Statistics show that only twenty four percent of emails are ever opened. A lessor percent of recipients read the messages on social media sites. Snail mail is better but does not assure a message is received, read, and understood.

With all of our technology, the most effective means of communications is meeting face to face, one on one.

An organization does not exist in isolation. It interacts with its environment. It is not a closed system. Closed systems operate with disregard for their environment while open systems interact with their environment - contributing and responding. Therefore, communications must be external as well as internal. External communications includes sales and marketing information and being a good citizen in the community, nation, and world. Major forms of external communication are product and institutional advertising. Product information includes product data, programs, and personnel. Institutional communications on the other hand creates a positive image of the organization and communicates the corporate values, priorities, and practices - the hidden things which create the organization's image.

Communication is dialog - sending and receiving, speaking and listening. Maintaining strong external communications must be a priority of the organization.

Jim was a veteran of World War II and a longtime friend. As a bombardier on a B-24, Jim flew many missions over Germany. We were having lunch one day at our favorite Mexican restaurant when I asked him the question which had been in my mind for a long time, "What was it like to be the one dropping bombs on German factories where there were people."

His reply was very interesting, "When I looked through the bomb-sight, I never saw people; only buildings and weapons factories."

Jim's statement had a tremendous impact on me. We all know that war is hell, and there are always going to be collateral damage, but that wasn't the point. Leaders normally are the ones with the long range view. In focusing on the goal/vision/purpose, there is a tendency to lose sight of our immediate surroundings; we may never see the people. I never want to get to the point where I do not see people.

So often we think we are doing our civic duty by sending a donation to the Salvation Army, overseas missionaries, or disaster relief. But without interacting directly with people, we are never doing enough. Something of the message is lost without a presence. It is the difference between being and doing. You can do great things, but it is more important to be great.

In the church, we tend to sit in our comfortable pew and send money for someone else to go into the poor neighborhoods of our cities, to go overseas and minister to people in the developing countries, or just to share our faith to our neighbors. But we will never receive the blessing of touching lives until we meet them face to face. That is a life changing event, not for the ones we touch, but for those who touch.

In the business world it is easier to sit in a comfortable chair behind our plush desk than it is to be out among the employees, customers, and the local community. The view from the office is a distorted image of the needs of the organization. There has to be a time to get away from all the hustle and bustle and take time to think and plan, but it is just as important to listen to what others are saying and be known to them.

In this TGIF world we live in there is so much technology at our disposal that there is a tendency to rely on these modern forms of communication to spread the word about the organization to literally millions of potential customers, investors, and the community. But that only works so far before it fails to close deals. There is still a need for face to face meetings between people, without telephones, or Skype. The most effective communications is still one on one. Studies have shown that what we say is not half as important as how we say it. People will interpret what we are communicating in three different ways; fifty five percent of what they hear is based upon our facial expression and body language, thirty seven percent is based upon the tone of our voice, and only eight percent on the words that we say.

Chapter 8 - Motivation

It happened just the way the coach had told us in preparation for the big game. The quarterback handed the football to the halfback who started to run around right end. Our defense reacted and followed the ball carrier. At that time I was the defensive end on the opposite side of the field, my coach's words stuck in my mind, "Don't be fooled, hold your ground, they will run a reverse."

Taking two steps across the line into the backfield, I stopped, watched, and waited. Sure enough, the halfback gave the ball off to the wide receiver on a reverse and he was coming straight at me - all alone on my side of the field. Everyone else had followed the halfback. It was just the two of us, and I was the only one that could prevent him from scoring. I held my ground, he tried to run around me, but I moved to intercept forcing him backwards. It was time to end this dance. Driving my shoulder into his midsection, I tackled him for an eight yard loss. That was one of my best days on the football field. The newspaper's article on the game finished with the line, "Johnson finally lived up to his potential."

"You have so much potential!" Those words are often meant to encourage, but they can also be a rebuke. The statement is a double edged sword. It encourages us to grow, become successful, and accomplish something great. As a rebuke, the statement says that you are not there yet, you have not lived up to your capabilities. It says you are not as good as you can be. Sadly most will never live up to their full potential. At the end of our lives we want to hear, "Well done!" but instead we often hear, "You had so much potential."

Why do some people exceed their potential, while others with the same capabilities and same history fall well short of what they could become?

117

Why is it that many people never realize their dreams and visions?

The answer is **<u>motivation</u>**.

In the field of sports, it is not the most gifted player that makes the hall of fame. In business, it is not the smartest person that builds the largest company. In a study of the Chief Executive Officers of Fortune 500 companies most were "C" average students. Motivation is the major factor that determines whether or not someone reaches their full potential. Organizations succeed or fail based upon motivation of the leadership, motivation of the workers, and motivation of the marketing force. Most leaders and experienced workers are good at specific tasks, but after many years in their position they become apathetic and lose their passion for their tasks.

Motivation is the reason or incentive to do something. It provides enthusiasm, interest, and commitment enables people to get up in the morning and go to work, not looking around for an excuse to stay home. Motivation keeps us going when things are tough.

What motivates you to be great?

What motivates you to be a leader?

What motivates you to build an organization?

If you are not properly motivated you may have a modicum of success but you will never reach your full potential. Leaders cannot motivate their followers if they themselves are lacking in proper motivation. Company presidents, medical professionals, organizational leaders, and church leaders primary goal is motivating others.

How can managers and leaders motivate their people to become more productive? How can we motivate our people to do more?

Needs Based Motivation

People are motivated, first, to meet their personal needs. American Psychologist, Abraham Maslow [44] developed a theory describing personal experiences. Maslow believed that humans strive for an upper level of capabilities. Humans seek the frontiers of creativity, the highest reaches of consciousness and wisdom. This is not a new concept. Plato, ancient Greek philosopher and founder of the Academy of Athens termed this state as "A fully Functioning Person." Today it is known by some as a healthy personality. Maslow used the phrase, "a self-actualizing person."

Maslow set up a hierarchy of five levels of basic needs. Beyond these needs, higher levels including needs for understanding, aesthetic appreciation, and purely spiritual needs. In fulfilling the five basic needs an individual does not move to the second need until the first is satisfied, nor does he move to the third until the second has been satisfied, and so on. Maslow's basic needs are pictured and described below:

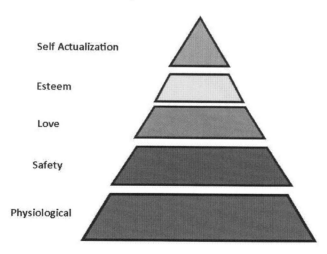

Physiological Needs: These are biological needs that a body needs to sustain life; oxygen, food, water, and a relatively

---

[44] Maslow, A.H. (1943). "A theory of human motivation." *Psychological Review, 50* (4), 370–96.

constant body temperature. Physiological needs are the first priority in one's search for satisfaction.

Safety Needs: When the physiological needs are satisfied and are no longer controlling thoughts and behaviors, security becomes the most important factor. With the rise in crime, terrorism, and wars around the world, security is a major issue and is high on everyone's priority list. Children often display the signs of insecurity and a need to be safe.

Need for Love, Affection, and Belonging: When the physiological and safety needs are satisfied Maslow states that the need for love, affection, and belonging emerge as a priority. People need to overcome their feelings of loneliness and alienation. This involves both giving and receiving love, affection, and the sense of belonging.

Need for Esteem: When the first three needs are satisfied, the need for esteem begins to dominate. Esteem involves both self-esteem and the esteem one receives from others. Human beings have a need for a stable, firmly based, high level of self-respect and respect from those around them. When these needs are satisfied, the person feels self-confident and valued. When these needs are frustrated, the person feels inferior, weak, helpless, and worthless.

Need for Self-Actualization: When all of the four previous needs are satisfied, then and only then is the need for self-actualization activated. Maslow describes self-actualization as a need to be and do that which the person was "born to do." It is their purpose in life, their personal vision of the future. "A musician must make music, an artist must paint, and a poet must write."

When needs are not met, they are felt in signs of restlessness. The person feels on edge, tense, and senses a lack of something. In short, they become restless. If a person is hungry, unsafe, not loved or accepted, or is lacking self-esteem, it is very easy to know what one is restless about.

The head of a medium sized services organization was having problems; morale was low, absenteeism was up, and the stability of the workforce was down. He called in an outside consultant for help and explained, "I can't get the people to do anything. They work here just for the paycheck."

The consultant met with several employees to get their input. Without the manager present, he interviewed supervisors and employees asking, "What do you think is the biggest problem with this company?"

Each responded similarly, "The boss won't let us do our job. He wants to micro-manage everything."

The consultant had heard this complaint many times before in other organizations. When things are not going right, managers often blame their people and the people blame their managers. It really does not matter who is right, what matters is the perception that one is right and one is wrong. The problem is one of motivation. Usually it is the leaders fault for failing to properly motivate his people. In fact, many techniques used by organizational leaders not only fail to motivate, but they discourage and de-motivate instead.

Motivation is a major issue in organizations that are not operating smoothly. If it is not a problem today, it will be a problem in the future.

Motivation comes from two places - outside or inside.

Extrinsic motivation comes from the outside; e.g. your mother threatens you with pain if you do not do your chores. The boss gives you a raise in pay if you do better on the job.

Intrinsic motivation comes from the inside; the feeling of accomplishment, the satisfaction of helping someone. Intrinsic motivation just makes you feel good.

Extrinsic Motivation

Money and other forms of reward are the most obvious examples of extrinsic motivation. Coercion and threat of punishment are also extrinsic motivations used by many. In sports, the crowd may cheer the athlete, and this motivates him or her to do well.

Trophies are also extrinsic incentives. Competition that encourages the athlete to win and reap the rewards is extrinsic, while competing to improve one's abilities can be intrinsic. There is a fine line the between the two. Extrinsic incentives often weaken motivation.

Studies[45] have shown that extrinsic motivation has seven deadly flaws.

- They can extinguish intrinsic motivation.
- They can diminish performance.
- They can crush creativity.
- They can crowd out good behavior.
- They can encourage cheating.
- They can become addictive.
- They can foster short-term thinking.

Intrinsic Motivation

Motivation has been studied by social and educational psychologists since the early 1970s. Research has found that intrinsic motivation is usually associated with high educational achievement and enjoyment by students. People are likely to be intrinsically motivated if they attribute their personal growth to internal factors that they can control, they believe they can be effective in reaching desired goals, and they are interested in

---

[45] Pink, Daniel H. (2009-12-24). Drive: The Surprising Truth About What Motivates Us (Kindle Locations 796-802). Penguin Group US. Kindle Edition.

mastering a task. This explains the "Starving Artist" or the writer that continues to write despite having no book sales.

Pink describes how traditional forms of motivation may, in some cases, decrease performance. He cites studies conducted with college students in the United States.

The researchers found that as long as the task required only mechanical or routine performance, extrinsic rewards worked well. Higher pay given for higher performance yielded better performance. Reward and punishment motivated the people when they were required to just follow the rules.

However, when the task became more complicated and required even a small bit of conceptual or creative thinking, extrinsic rewards failed to motivate and even reduced levels of performance. Higher pay for solving puzzles, for creative thinking, and for more complicated tasks had a negative effect on performance. There was a concern that American college students were not representative of a complete society. So the researchers moved their testing to Madurai, India. The villagers were given similar tests and the results were consistent despite the obvious cultural differences.

According to Pink there are three major intrinsic factors which have the power to motivate individuals engaged in other than routine tasks;

- autonomy,

- mastery,

- and purpose.

Autonomy

As the San Diego technical services company grew from two into an organization, structure had to be added to accommodate the mission. It was time to start delegating. There would be no time for the leader to control everything. Responsibility and authority had to be shared. That is not an easy task for a leader that likes to be in control. The leader must accept the fact that someone else might do the same task differently. If the organization were to succeed, the employees must be free to perform their tasks with a certain amount of autonomy. They needed to be free to make mistakes and learn from their mistakes. The leader is still be required to guide and teach, but not command and control. Creativity and motivation flow like a river. The leader can provide levees to channel the water but should not be a dam which stops the flow.

This was accomplished best by:

- Assigning the task

- Discussing methods of approach

- Regularly reviewing progress.

- Being available to provide additional resources and aid.

But what happens if the job is really boring? How do we motivate someone? Pink suggests three methods:

- Offer a rationale for why the task is necessary. A job that's not inherently interesting can become more meaningful, and therefore more engaging, if it's part of a larger purpose.

- Acknowledge that the task is boring. This is an act of empathy, of course.

- Allow people to complete the task their own way. Think autonomy, not control. State the outcome you need, instead of specifying precisely the way to achieve reach it.

In today's Post-Modern society, autonomy is a strong motivator. People want to feel they have ownership and control over their lives. They want to control their own destiny. They are less likely to accept authoritarian leadership. But personal autonomy as a motivator is not new. Each of us has a desire to be self-directed. Traditional management techniques demand compliance. But if you want engagement, self-direction is a better motivator.

In his 1985 book,"[46] author and ministry leader Frank R. Tillapaugh, describes how his church grew to provide a powerful outreach to his community. When someone came to him with a concern for a certain people group or community, they would often say, "Someone ought to do something." Tillapaugh would then encourage the person with the concern to research what was needed, what was currently available, and figure out what could be done in the future to provide help. Tillapaugh provided resources and advice, but he released them to start and lead a new program. He provided resources and guidance but gave them complete autonomy. While some of these outreaches failed, many more became successful and expanded the impact of the ministry in the community.

While managers often tend toward controlling their organizations as a means to eliminate costly mistakes and improve efficiency, a catalytic leader will empower his people to become all that they can be. Giving people autonomy allows them to make mistakes and grow from their experience. There is no greater teacher than failure.

Mastery

The saddest sentence in the world is: "I am not good at anything."

In the fifth grade Rhonda was an average student, working hard in school. Like most pre-teens it was difficult every morning to get her up and off to school. Then one day she came home and announced she wanted to play the flute in the school band. Up until then she had no musical ambitions

---

[46] Tillapaugh, Frank R. Unleashing the Church, getting people out of the fortress into ministry, Regal Books, 1982, Ventura, CA

other than dancing classes. As she continued her flute lessons, her whole attitude toward school changed. Now she was up early and in a hurry to get off to school. She enjoyed being in the band and growing in her musical abilities. One summer she attended band camp and continued to master her music. Mastery of her instrument and music was the motivator that gave her a new perspective about school.

Rita dreamed of becoming an oil painter but lacked the confidence to pursue the art. An ad in the local newspaper for a class in oil painting caught her eye. It read, "NO Experience Necessary." For the next several years she was motivated by the challenge to master the art of painting in oils. On the day of her class day there was hardly anything that could stop her from getting to class to become more proficient. Today, her oil paintings are displayed collections throughout the world and she has her own studio and teaches aspiring artists. As she teaches, Rita's mastery continues to increase. She continues to be motivated to grow and learn.

There are thousands of amateur musicians who practice daily and sometimes play gigs on weekends. Why do they do it? It does not support them. They do it because they enjoy playing and face the continual challenge of mastering their art. It has been said that a musician is someone that takes a $3,000 instrument, puts it in a $1,000 car and drives to a gig where they earns $30.

Mastery is the urge to improve ourselves. It does not matter whether it is playing an instrument, teaching a class, or digging a ditch. Human beings have this deep-seated desire to master something. Motivation to work harder comes from the desire to become excellent at something.

In his book "Outliers: The Story of Success," author Malcolm Gladwell writes;

The idea that excellence at performing a complex task requires a critical minimum level of practice surfaces

126

again and again in studies of expertise. In fact, researchers have settled on what they believe is the magic number for true expertise: ten thousand hours.[47]

Gladwell cites several examples including the Beatles who accumulated their 10,000 hours playing where ever they could find a spot, playing for extended hours, under difficult conditions, and for little or no money just because they were motivated to master their art. It was only after all that work that they became famous.

Organizations develop motivated workers by providing opportunities for growth and development to help them master their craft. Many companies provide paid tuition and bonuses for employees to grow by taking formal education classes or in-house training programs and seminars where outside experts are used train.

When people stop growing, they lose their motivation.

Significance

Somewhere in a person's life they come to a point where they question themselves and ponder where they are in their life. Many books and articles have been written about this time and have given it the popular name of "Midlife Crisis." It doesn't always happen at midlife, but somewhere along the line we realize that our life should have more significance. Everyone would like to believe that their life has meaning and significance. We all want to know that what we do with the time given to us on this earth is important. In business and politics the word "legacy" is bandied about as if a person's life could be summed up by what he or she leaves behind. Each of us will leave a legacy and we want it to have meant something. We all cannot be president of the United States, a great athlete

---

[47] Gladwell, Malcolm (2008-10-29). Outliers: The Story of Success (pp. 39-40), Little, Brown, and Company.

with gold medals, or even the head of a large company. We can, however have a life filled with meaning and significance.

I once knew a man who dug ditches for a living. There were some who looked down on him because of his job and the dirt that clung to his cloths after a day in toiling in mud. But I admired him because he sought excellence in digging ditches. He knew the importance of each ditch that he dug. His ditches carried away rain water saving communities from flooding. His ditches provided sanitary removal of human waste which prevented disease and epidemics. His ditches were used to provide fresh water to houses all over town. His task as a ditch digger had more significance than that of many of his critics.

In an organization there are many levels of workers from the top leader to the person that cleans the toilets. Each one can be motivated if they feel their particular job is important. Leaders must let everyone know how important their particular job will be to the success of the organization. Realizing the significance of one's position will motivate each one to do their very best in each situation.

But, how does the president of a manufacturing company convince an assembly line worker that his role is significant? How does the chairman of the board of a software company convince the janitor that his job is significant?

There are three primary steps that will convince people that their position and task has significance:

1. The leaders themselves must be convinced that their organization has a significant role to fulfill in society. They must understand that it is not about making a profit; it is about providing a product or a service which is significant and meaningful to the world outside of the organization.

2. Leaders at every level must be convinced of the significance of their own particular role in the organization.

3. When new employees are hired or new members join, they must be convinced of the importance of organization's products and services, and the importance of their particular role to which they will be assigned. Each one must be convinced to seek excellence in performing his or her function.

If the top managers do not feel the significance of their organization, its products, and services, they should not be filling these positions. If they are just in it for the prestige, money, or power, they will be ineffective in truly leading the organization. When middle managers, production line workers and janitors detect the insincerity of the top managers, they will not give their best efforts.

Bessie, at age seventy five, was one of the happiest people alive. Each morning she opened her eyes and thanked God for another day. When you met her on the street she seemed to bubble with joy and excitement. It seemed totally out of place for someone dying of an incurable disease. She had accepted her condition and knew it was only a matter of time when her eyes would be closed forever. She took radiation and Chemo-Therapy treatments regularly leaving her tired and keeping her from even simple physical tasks. One morning after her treatment at the local hospital, Bessie came into my office and literally flopped into the visitor's chair. There was something different in her eyes today. This was the first time I had ever seen her sad. She seemed almost depressed. My mind began to race with thoughts of bad news from her doctors.

Heaving a deep sigh of resignation, Bessie spoke very subdued, "I have just come from the cancer ward. There are so many patients and families there that are confused, worried, and desperate. It is so sad. My heart is breaking for them and I don't know what I can do about it. I feel the need to pray for them, cheer them up, and minister to their families. But I don't know how or what to do."

After considering her concern, I gave her an assignment, "Bessie, the first thing you need is the permission from the hospital. They have strict rules about who can approach patients in treatment rooms. They have had some bad experiences with some well-meaning people in the past. I'll call the Director of Patient Services and make an appointment for you. She is the only one with the authority to give you permission. Then explain to her what you want to do."

A couple of days later Bessie burst into my office with a big grin on her face. "They told me I could do it." She paused and looked confused, "But, what do I do now? Where do I start?"

We discussed ways to approach the patients and decided to just follow the leading of the Spirit.

After two years of ministry to cancer patients and their families Bessie succumbed to her own cancer leaving behind a legacy of, cancer survivors, thankful families, amazed doctors and nurses, and a treatment room that had been transformed from a dark and deathly cell into a place of hope, peace, and thanksgiving even in the midst of sorrow and uncertainty.

Bessie, at age seventy five found significance.

Chapter 9 - Planning

Business plans are the promise of a future. Newly founded organizations often put together a business plan which may be required by incorporation agencies, board members, banks, investors, and officers to demonstrate that the founders know what they are doing; that they have a plan, they have a direction, and a reasonably good chance of success in their endeavor. We have had the challenge of creating many business plans and opportunity to evaluate at least five times as many plans in evaluating acquisition candidates.

Non-profit organizations are not immune from the need for business planning although the details of their plans will have a different emphasis.

There is a common pattern in most business plans; a voluminous amount of financial forecast, market data, and organizational details. Most plans will go unread by investors, but kept in the files in the event of a problem or if someone asks a question. What the plan says is not as important as the fact that a plan exists. Most of the people that require plans just want to know that there is a plan. That is why it was refreshing to hear the account of the launching of the tremendously successful film production company *Dream Works*. According to Jeffrey Katzenberg, their business plan was written on a single page.

Dream Works produced the film, "Prince of Egypt," based upon the story of Moses. Born into a Jewish family, Moses was given up by his mother to protect his life, and raised by an Egyptian Princess. The child and his step brother grew up together as brothers and both became princes of Egypt. When Moses was forty years old, he witnessed the cruelty the Jews faced at the hands of the Egyptians. Later Moses killed one of the slave drivers. This caused him to flee to the desert where he lived for another forty years tending sheep until God called him to deliver the Hebrews out of slavery into the Promised Land.

Dream Works wanted to make sure the movie was accurate and not be offensive to any religious group, so they invited several religious leaders to view the movie before it was released.

During the showing of the film, Katzenberg made the statement, "The Prince of Egypt movie is the story of 'Dream Works.'" He went on to explain, "Moses spent forty years as a prince in Egypt, learning leadership principles. Then he spent forty years learning desert survival. When he was prepared for his life purpose, God called him and used him."

Dream Works was founded by three men: Steven Spielberg, the greatest movie story teller; Jeffrey Katzenberg, the greatest animation story teller; and David Geffen, the greatest musical story teller. Each one had been preparing themselves. When they came together to found the company, their business plan consisted of one single page. Rather than planning for the launch of the new company, the three partners had been preparing themselves for years.

Planning is important, but preparation is more important. We have to make ourselves ready to take on the tasks to which we have been called. According to Malcolm Gladwell, successful preparation will take about ten thousand hours.[48] In his book "Outliers, the story of success, Gladwell sites several instances of athletes, musicians, lawyers and business executives who were prepared for that day when

---

[48] Gladwell, Malcolm (2008-10-29). Outliers: The Story of Success

success came to them. In his research it appears to Gladwell that ten thousand hours of preparation are required for success.

Investors, partners, and associates are more concerned whether the founders of an organization are prepared to build their organizations than the details of the business plan. A good business plan should demonstrate this preparedness.

Planning for the Future

If you ask one hundred men at age twenty five if they plan to be successful in life most would say, "Yes." Then at the age of sixty five, one will be rich, four will be financially independent, five will still be working and fifty four will be broke." Earl Nightingale[49]

Why do they fail? The opposite of courage is not cowardice; it is conformity. That is the trouble today, conformity; everyone is acting the same as everyone else without knowing why nor where they are going. Why do they conform?

They believe their lives are controlled by external forces that they have no control over. Determinism has led to the "Occupy" movements and much of the antiestablishment movements on college campuses and in the public square. If you ask the protesters why they are protesting, most cannot describe it accurately, but they are just dissatisfied with their lives and did not see any hope. Rather than believe that they might be wrong, they look for someone else that they can blame their situation - someone that might be successful.

To them it is a zero sum game. If someone gains someone else has to lose. It is all a matter of luck, if someone wins life's lottery, everyone else loses. If the total gains of the participants are added up and the total losses are subtracted, they will sum to zero. It is as if there is only one cake and if I

---

[49] Nightingale, Earl, *The Strangest Secret*, Ophelia Madison Press, Hagerstown MD

eat more than my share someone else will suffer. Determinism leads to hopelessness resulting in anger, anxiety, and defeatism. The only solution they see is to strike out at authorities, the successful, and the system they believe caused their condition. There are times when each of us might fall prey to a deterministic hopelessness.

The solution is finding hope in the future. Determine what you want to achieve, and make that your long range goal in life. You may not know how to get there, but we all need a significant goal to get us up and going every day. It is the same for an business, service, or religious organization. There must be a long range goal. Success is not always achieving the goal. Success is merely progressing towards the goal.

But Success is the school teacher who is teaching school because she has a passion for seeing children grow; the wife and mother that wants that to be her role; the man who runs the corner gas station because that is what he always wanted to do; the one that digs ditches and is happy with his purpose. Success is anyone who is doing the something because that is what he deliberately decided to do. But only one out of twenty people in our nation are doing what they really want to do.

Organizations are similar to individuals. They need that significant purpose in life. Like the protesters on Wall Street who need to understand that they need to have a goal and a plan to achieve it, organizations must keep an eye to the future in order to know what to do today.

As product manager at a small manufacturing company in the Deep South, I was concerned that the organization was merely reacting to business conditions. There was no strategic plan. Walking into the office of the vice president and I said, "We need a five year plan and I want to prepare one." He looked at me like a parent would whose child had just asked for his allowance to be doubled.

"We don't need any five year plan," he railed, "We don't even know whether we will be here in five years."

Under my breath I said, "We won't be here in five years unless we plan now."

We did not talk about the five year plan again until the day I presented the finished plan. As a result of the plan we developed and introduced new products and new markets had opened up for us.

The key question:

"What is your long range vision for this organization?"

While we cannot always predict the future, it is possible to describe our concept of what we would like things to be like and what it will be doing in the coming years.

Organizations must have a collective goal in order to be called an "organization." In order for that organization to become successful, it must have a significant collective goal. That is why we spend so much time and energy discussing, purpose, vision, and mission. The major question for the entrepreneur is , "What will be the purpose of your organization?"

The following questions must be answered in order to define the vision.

What will be the primary products and services in five years?

Who will be your primary customers and clients for those products and services?

What will be the geographical coverage of your organization?

Why would someone select your organization for their requirements?

How big will the organization be in five years?

- In the size of the staff

- The volume of business

- Members, Customer or clients

What outstanding characteristics will distinguish you in the eyes of your members, clients and competitors?

What factors can you foresee that would impact your organization?

What are the top practices of your organization that will fulfill your vision?

In developing a corporate plan it is important to always define accurately the purpose, vision, and mission. The purpose statement will contain two or three elements or phrases.

What will the organization do?

What significant things will result for:

- The community/customers/clients

- The organization

- The employees or members

- Other stakeholders

What are the core values and priorities which drive the answers to the above questions?

Just the act of developing a long range plan will significantly improve the chances of success for any organization for a time. But plans are not cast in concrete.

Setting Goals

"I can't say I was ever lost, but I was bewildered once for three days." [Daniel Boone]

After four weeks of training a group of officer candidates were on an exercise in the woods at a far corner of the Fort Gordon Army Base near Augusta Georgia. These four weeks provided intense classroom and field training. The field training often simulated actual combat situations.

Now on this dark, moonless night, our unit was divided into groups of three, taken deep into an area of overgrown woods, swamp and heavy brush As we were dropped off we were given a map, a compass and a white handkerchief and instructed to find our way to a rendezvous point some two miles away. We were lost. We had never been in this spot before nor had we ever been to the rendezvous point. They were just two X's on a map. There were no GPS devices, cell phones, nor flashlights.

Our mission was to find our way through the woods, underbrush, and swamp - without the aid of any light - to our goal where we would meet up with the other teams. Did I say it was a dark, moonless night? Before we were dropped off, we were able to look at the map and find the range and bearing to the rendezvous point. For us it was two miles to the Southwest, or 225° on the compass. Coming in last was not an option. The team that finished last would not get a weekend pass. This exercise was somewhat akin to the TV show, "The Great Race."

Earlier that day we had practiced night vision in a "Dark Room." One of the most amazing things about our eyes is their incredible dynamic range. We can see in very bright sunlight, and we can also see in nearly total darkness. New digital cameras seem to have the ability to amplify or attenuate light so the picture becomes clear. Our eyes have a similar feature. The dynamic range of our eyes results from three different parts of the eye: pupil, rods, and cones. In our biological night vision, molecules of rhodopsin in the rods of the eye undergo a change in shape as they absorb light. Rhodopsin is the chemical that allows night-vision, and is extremely sensitive to light. Exposed to a spectrum of light, the pigment immediately bleaches, and it takes about thirty minutes to regenerate fully, but most of the adaptation occurs within the first five or ten minutes in the dark. Rhodopsin in the human rods is less sensitive to the longer red wavelengths of light, so traditionally many people use red light to help preserve night vision as it only slowly depletes the eye's rhodopsin stored in the rods and instead is viewed by the cones.

At the drop-off point we waited for our night vision to begin. When our eyes adjusted, we used the compass with its slightly glowing dial to determine the direction we were to head. Walking straight was impossible due to the trees and underbrush. So we sent one person ahead with the white handkerchief as a marker. In the almost total darkness, with our now increased night vision, we could see the handkerchief at distances of between fifteen and thirty feet. Using the compass, we positioned the handkerchief carrier to a spot in line with our ultimate destination. The handkerchief provided a near term goal that we could see and achieve. Once reaching the handkerchief the plan was repeated as a new goal was set. Each time the handkerchief carrier would go just far enough that we could still make out his white cloth. Continuing to repeat this process for the two miles, we waded through swamps and around trees and finally achieved our objective. We were not last.

This training exercise taught me several things about setting goals.

1. Before you set your goals, you have to know where you are right now.

2. Before you set any goals, you have to know where you want to end up.

3. When you set a goal, it must be in alignment with your ultimate destination.

4. Even though you may not be able to see the ultimate destination, you have to be able to see the goal from your current location.

5. The path to your next goal may be fraught with hidden perils: swamps, forests, and angry dogs,

6. You must keep your goal in sight and be unwavering in your quest.

7. You must take the first step toward your intermediate goal.

Is there a key to success? You will notice that some people just continue to fail, while others continue to succeed. Some fail and then get back up and succeed. Earl Nightingale - writer, respected speaker and author, dealing mostly on the subjects of human character development, motivation, excellence and meaningful existence; so named as the "Dean of Personal Development," says it is because of goals. Some have them; some do not. Think of a ship sailing out of a harbor with no destination. The ship will go where ever the winds blow. The key to success and the key to failure is that we become what we think about.

Marcus Aurelius was the last of the five "Good" Roman emperors. He ruled from 161 to 180 AD and was considered one of the most important of the Stoic Philosophers. He wrote,

"A man's life is what his thoughts make of it."

Ralph Waldo Emerson writes,

"A man is what he thinks about all day long."

We become what we think about. If a farmer plants a field with corn, he will have a great crop of corn in the fall. If he plants weeds in the field, when fall comes he will have nothing but weeds. We are like the farmer and our minds are like the fields. What we plant in our minds is what we will eventually harvest. We will reap what we have sown.

Our mind does not care what we plant; it will return anything we plant. Our mind is free, and we are the sum total of all our thoughts. We are guided by our minds. A huge earth moving machine has only a tiny driver. Our mind is that tiny driver. Isaac Newton's third law of motion applies here - "For every action there is an equal and opposite reaction."

The strangest secret in the world, according to Earl Nightingale, is that we become what we focus our attention on. If we focus on our fears, we will never be able to get out of bed in the morning, but if we focus on our goals and purpose we arise excited anticipating the new day. Nightingale, in "The Strangest Secret," identifies three steps to changing your life:

- Write down what you want more than anything else.

- Stop thinking about what you fear.

- Your success will always be measured by the quality and quantity of the service you render.

If you want to fulfill your purpose, start to focus on your goals, stop focusing on your fears, and take the next right step toward your destiny.

While Nightingale was writing about personal success, his insight can also be applied to an organization.

Earlier we considered the long range vision and purpose of the organization. Now it is time to identify near term goals that will lead us toward our ultimate destination, our vision, and our purpose. That is our rendezvous point. Once there is a statement of purpose. Action and discipline are required to pursue the vision. Success is the progressive realization of a worthy ideal. Success is to continue to see and get to the white cloth just ahead in the dark night. If someone is working toward a predetermined goal and knows where they are going, they are a success. Who succeeds? The one pursuing a worthy ideal who says, "I want to be this," and then begins to work toward that goal. That is the one who often succeeds.

Along the way we need to evaluate our progress, our strengths, and our weaknesses which may cause us to adjust our immediate goals. Goals should be written so you can evaluate your progress. It is too easy to forget them once you have them established. Put a "Post It" note on your mirror if you have to, so you can look at it every morning. Think about your future destiny every day. Understand that you become what think about.

Cut loose of what holds you back. Be free to imagine what you can do. All you need is to have a purpose and faith. Fear will cause you to fail. Doubt in the heart will ruin your opportunities to be effective.

Interstate Highway H-3 opened on December 12, 1997 after twenty years of technical, environmental, and political problems. The highway connects the naval base at Pearl Harbor with the Naval Air Station in Kaneohe on the North Shore. The Highway tunnels through the Ko'olau Mountains exiting several hundred feet above the Haiku Valley then a viaduct carries the traffic down to the Likelike Highway.

In 1991 it became my task to investigate the highway contractor's concerns about radiation from the Coast Guard navigational system antenna which threatened construction equipment and construction workers in the intense field of the antenna.

The first afternoon on site was spent surveying the task. Only one lane of the viaduct was under construction and looked like a giant diving board extending about two hundred feet out from the mountain side and about two hundred feet above the valley floor. My job was to move out to the end of the last segment of the viaduct and make measurements. I began to panic. My fear of heights and my fear of bridges caused me to shudder just thinking about spending all of the next day on the end of the pirate's plank.

I drove to the site praying after an anxious night with little sleep. Nearing the construction zone, it seemed the Lord was reassuring me, "Keep your eyes focused on your work and not the danger around you."

Going out to the end of the viaduct and returning to the mountain was scary; however, all that day, as I focused on my work, my fears totally disappeared. When taking a break I was even able to enjoy the awesome view of Kaneohe Bay with the ocean beyond and the lush jungle greenery of the Haiku Valley below.

> *Our doubts are traitors, and make us lose the good we oft might win by fearing to attempt. (William Shakespeare)*

Dr. Norman Vincent Peale wrote

> *This is one of the greatest laws of the universe...my greatest discovery outside of my relationship with God; if you think in negative terms you will get negative*

results, if you think in positive terms you will get positive results. Believe and succeed.

Do these three things:

1. Think about where you are heading;

2. Do not think about the things you fear.

3. Do the things that will move you forward towards your destiny.

Then you will be well on the road to living up to your potential and becoming the person God created you to be.

Evaluating Progress

Each organization will have a unique purpose, mission, and vision. For many the desired result is financial. This is the case in many for-profit business organizations. Certainly in the stock market success is measured in terms of earnings and return on investment. The price of a share of stock rises and falls with only a small fluctuation in earnings. If the corporation fails to meet projected earnings it is considered a failure and its stock price drops. By this, the measurement of a business organization's effectiveness is in the price of its stock.

But we know that stock markets are volatile and often respond emotionally to such things as war, geophysical events, and political elections. Therefore the stock price is not always a good measurement of the effectiveness of business organizations. Not-for-profit and benevolent organizations would not be able to use this scale to measure effectiveness. Still non-profits require funding sources and supporters to finance their activities. There are many non-profit entities that measure their success based upon the amount of revenue they receive, when actually the measurement of their success is how many people they help or how much good they do for the world. Financial details enter in as a measure of effectiveness, in all organizations because it is a quantifiable metric.

The true measure of effectiveness is achieving the desired result, progressing toward the ultimate purpose or rendezvous point. Unlike financial data of organizations, the effectiveness of organization priorities, practices, and programs is more subjective than and less objective. Some of the most important elements of an organization, being subjective are not easily evaluated.

The first step in measuring effectiveness is to list every goal that has been established and chart its progress. A spread sheet, Gantt chart or other means can be used to plot progress. For financial campaigns a "thermometer chart" is often used. This will quickly reveal when there are problems in completing a goal on schedule.

But how do we measure important organizational elements such as priorities, practices, and programs that are subjective in nature? These elements are significant because they will impact the achievement of our goals and vision. Any change in priorities, practices, and programs will be a precursor of a change in the ability to complete goals. An evaluation should be completed regularly to keep the organization on track.

A non-profit organization was having relational problems throughout the organization. There was a lot of bickering and not much respect shown for leadership and other member and workers. Yet one of the organization's identified core values was "respect for others." A special leadership meeting was called. The meeting was open to all levels of leadership. The meeting began with two questions:

What have we been doing right and what areas do we need to improve upon?

The attendees were divided into groups of five or six people who were instructed to work together and provide answers to the proposed questions. As the small groups came back with their answers, each was given the opportunity to

144

share their response. The responses to the first question varied but focused on a few different areas. The second question, however, had unanimous agreement. The answer was that there needed to be improvement in dealing with each other. There was a lack of respect throughout the organization.

After returning to the small groups, each team was asked to come up with suggestions as to how they might resolve the respect issue and change the working atmosphere of the organization. Each small group made several recommendations. The recommendations were then published throughout the company, but no official rule changes were adopted by top management.

A year later, another meeting was held that opened with the same two questions:

"What are we doing right and what needs improvement?"

After conferring in small groups the answers were given. The issue of respect was still unanimous. The difference was that this time it was the answer to the first question, "What are we doing right?"

It is interesting that after the original meeting, the recommendations by the groups were not codified in any manner. There was no memo to the organization. There were on speeches on the subject. There were no posters on the wall. What changed were the values of the individuals. They took ownership of the problem and they took ownership of the solution. As this group of leaders consciously changed their priorities and practices, almost everyone in the organization also changed. As a result, corporate values changed in less than a year.

This story illustrates two specific ideas: First; subjective elements of an organization such as values, priorities, and practices can be accurately evaluated; and second, the use of

145

subjective opinion can be used as an objective measurement in evaluating the effectiveness of an organization.

Businesses, political parties, and governments have come to rely on polls to determine how well they are doing. Every day with emails from E-commerce organizations as well as traditional companies with Internet capabilities. In the continuous campaign seasons we see daily polls of who is more popular. Politicians often use this data to promote policies and legislation. We are hit with news items about the popularity of the president, the congress, or some government agency. These are equated to a predominately subjective evaluation of how well someone is doing in their position.

Organizations which provide products or services use surveys to detect potential problems before they get out of hand. What is the health of the organization? What are the strengths and weaknesses of all facets of an organization? Here are some questions to ask in your organization.

1. How effective is the current organizational "Structure" to fulfill its mission?

2. Is the "Corporate Culture" conducive to growth?

3. Is the leadership capable of taking the organization into the future?

4. How well do the individual "Department" leaders function?

5. Resources

6. Are "Employee" capabilities adequate?

7. How well do we "Communicate?"

8. Do we have the needed "Technology?"

9. Are the "Facilities" adequate?

The following is an example of using subjective attitudes to evaluate your organization. This assessment of the current status of the organization should be done using the team approach with each participant rating the organization on a scale of 1 – 10. (1 = poor and 10 = excellent.) Once the groups have completed their evaluation, the results can be averaged and formed into a graph giving a visual presentation. We used a "Radar" graph.

Structure	9
Corporate culture	4
Executive leadership	6
Department leadership	5
Employee capability	6
Communications	4
Technology	8
Facilities	1

The results of our sample evaluation are shown in the radar graph. This graph points out quickly the areas that need help.

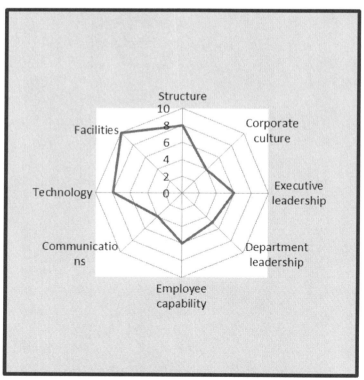

Just a quick look at this assessment indicates that the organization has some real problems, which would appear to originate with the leadership. While this organization and the evaluation were purely mythical, not representing any know entity, it is interesting that the results would indicate the company has reached the point where the vision has been lost and leaders seem oblivious to the situation.

The results of the evaluation reflect that leadership is marginal and the company has moved into the "Institutionalization" cycle and requires structural changes to break out into a more productive mode.

An organization in the Western United States developed a questionnaire that could be used for their specific type of organization. It listed thirty two different practices of the organization and asked the respondents to rate the organization's effectiveness on a scale from one to five with (5) being the best and (1) being the worst. The questionnaire included demographic data which was later used to compare the resulting data with organizations with similar demographics. With a data base of nearly a thousand organizations they were able to compare responses and provide a good assessment of an organization's effectiveness. It was interesting to note that of those organizations which were growing substantially the highest rated practice was providing a clear focused purpose.

Every business organization has core values, priorities and practices which are in place to support the basic purpose of the organization. The basic health of the business can be evaluated by measuring how effective the company is in living up to its values, priorities and practices.

As an example, if XYZ Company has a core value of financial security, with a priority of immediate profitability and return on investment, you might want to look at the bottom line of its financial report for an indication of its health. What you do not know from this is whether the company is sacrificing its future for immediate profits in place of investing in research and development and opening new markets with new products. The higher profits and dividends will often increase the stock price rise temporarily at the sacrifice of the future. While I was in the position of evaluating potential acquisition candidates it was interesting that most of them attempted to inflate the financial bottom line in a move to increase their position before the merger. Unless the acquiring company is looking for a tax write off, it must be very careful when analyzing candidates.

In order for an organization to succeed it must keep accurate statistics of both successes and failures. Profit and loss is important, but it is not the primary means of measuring the success of an organization. We can only look at Amazon's first four years to prove that. Finances are not a measurement of the dynamism of the organization, but they reveal data which can be used to correct and adjust practices.

Most successful companies invest in the future by putting profits back into the organization to stimulate future growth. The economies of the world have been damaged in recent years by an overemphasis on the bottom line. Giant corporations, banks, and real estate brokerages have taken put money into profits which should have been used for research and development, opening new markets, and altruistic goals.

Go you have to change? In order to determine what and how much we need to change, it is important to review our organizational, values, priorities, practices, personnel, and programs.

Values: What are the organization's current core values? Have they changed in the past? Why have they changed? What are your personal values?

Priorities/Vision/Mission: List your priorities in order of importance. Which of these are in line with your core values? Have you changed your priorities to meet or compete?

149

Practices, (Form VS Function): Are your practices leading you to your vision/mission/purpose? Are the practices mere ritual or habit? Or are they still vital and productive?

Personnel: Do you have the right personnel in place to fulfill the practices? Are they properly motivated? Are they well trained?

Programs: How do you select programs? Do you copy what has worked in other organizations, reinvented your own, or developed a hybrid based upon your own Values, Priorities, and Practices?

When the organization's purpose, values and priorities have been identified, its practices are the means to move from today's situation to the future. The route to the future begins at the current point at which the organization exists. Therefore it is important identify exactly where the organization is today. In some organizations forecasting is merely wishful thinking. It may have no basis in fact or in conditions, but is merely a rough estimate by the forecaster, or worse.

Business forecasting is a vital factor in all organizations. Forecasts are used to position resources, set manpower levels, and establish a standard against which results will be measured. The accuracy of the forecast will have a huge impact on profitability, employment, and the price of the company's stock.

As we look at the stock market activity for a share of a business, the price of its stock is often set by the predicted gains and losses. When the forecasts are not met, the stock price is affected and investors lose confidence in the management of the company. Many officers of corporations lose their jobs over inaccurate forecasts.

In Not-For-Prophet entities, relying on donations from supporters, budgets are made based on anticipated income. The forecasts must be accurate in order to properly manage and lead any organization. Estimating too low an income is almost as bad as estimating too large an income. Forecasting affects the success of every organization.

Forecasting Methodology

As we have observed forecasting over the past thirty some years we have seen a great disparity between the accuracy of several different methods. The following methods are typically used by organizations of all types and sizes.

Historically Based:

Often forecasts will be based upon previous years' results with a slight increase based upon the national inflation rate. This assumes that nothing will change in the organization and its market place and the most used method. But it will only work for organizations that are very stable and there are no changes in the economy, and the organization's products and market position is not changing. My first forecast as a marketing director used the historical method with some modifications. I was able to factor in the anticipated impact of my changes that we were incorporation. If I remember correctly my estimates for the immediate future were somewhat high but correct in the out years. Being young, I was over optimistic about the time it would take to make changes.

The Dreamer Approach:

This type of forecast is made by supreme optimists. They look at all the possibilities of new customers, new products and/or new services. They do not anticipate any problems. The dreamer will overestimate the size of the market size and his share of that market.

The Pessimist's Approach:

This is the opposite of the dreamer approach. The pessimist uses the worst case scenarios in all aspects; the economy will tank, new product development will be delayed, and we will lose customers.

Scientific Approach:

A more realistic approach to organizational forecasting would include;

- Demographic analysis: Who are the people we are serving, where are they , and how can we best provide for their needs>

- Market studies: How big is the market? What do our clients need? What is our percentage of the current market? What political, economic, or industry factors will affect the market? Will the market be growing or declining? Who are our competitors? What are our competitors doing to win clients? Etc.

- Social trends: What are the social trends which will impact the market and our position in the market?

- Analysis of the organization's strengths and weaknesses: Where will we put new resources, to strengthen weaknesses or improve strengths? Sometimes it may be more advantageous to improve strengths than to solve weaknesses. The analysis of the organization's strengths and weaknesses would include its place in the organizational life cycle.

In the initial structuring phase of the company's life cycle, the ability to adapt to changing conditions provides great opportunities and can lead to accelerated growth. At the same time mistakes made are more costly and could result in a rapid decline in profitability. In this phase of the company's life cycle everything is extremely volatile.

When the organization reaches the maximum efficiency phase it would be very hard to change and as a result, the forecasting becomes easier.

Growth Factors

A statistical analysis of non-manufacturing organizations demonstrates that the following factors tend to increase organizational growth.

- Knowledge of organization's purpose is the number one factor in determining growth.

- Established Goals

- Need based marketing,

- Cooperative decision making.

- Strong leadership.

- Employees or members feel their job has significance.

Chapter 10 - Do You Want Change?

As this chapter is being written, our region of the country, like many others is suffering from a long draught. My grass has turned to a grayish brown, the hedge is turning yellow, and the leaves of the azaleas are wilting. Still I know that the roots remain strong and when the rains return and we apply fertilizer, the yard will return to its pre-draught beauty. It is the same for an organization which has been suffering from a lack of sustenance. There is a change coming. But what do we change and how do we make changes without destroying the organization? The first task is to reexamine all aspects of the organization.

Are you satisfied with the progress and direction of your organization, corporation, or government? If your answer is yes, there is nothing else to do. But if you have gotten this far in the book, you probably are dissatisfied with some aspect of your organization and want to make changes. As we take an objective look at the organization, we must ask whether it is moving toward the vision for which it was created, and if not, why not? There may be valid reasons for a change in vision, such as a realization that your personal values and priorities have changed.

The word, "Change" seems to evoke many different emotions. We often as a pointed question at leadership retreats,

"When you hear the word 'Change' what feelings does it evoke inside of you?"

Some admit to a sense of fear of the unknown, while others have a positive reaction and are excited about new opportunities. Organizational change will result in both fear and anticipation in different individuals.

Change results in chaos, or change occurs in response to chaos. Whichever comes first the two are inseparable. Change and chaos go together. Chaos theory concerns deterministic

155

systems whose behavior can in principle be predicted. Chaotic systems are predictable for a while and then appear to become random. Chaos theory, sometimes referred to as the "Butterfly Effect," refers to the effect of small changes which have a large impact. In common usage, "chaos" means "a state of disorder. In organizations, we frequently experience chaotic effects. A casual comment made at a meeting takes on a life of its own and runs through the organization causing chaos.

Change is usually in response to certain issues, disorders which must be corrected and require action or movement. When things move, inertia must be overcome and friction will exist. Movement plus friction results in heat. That means conflict is inevitable. Change is also exciting, something new is coming. But change is scary because it disrupts the status quo. In order to do something different, we will have to let go of something that we don't feel comfortable losing.

There is the story told of a man that fell off the cliff and grabbed on to a slim tree branch that kept him from falling to the rocks below. There he was suspended in midair with only the small branch keeping him from sure death. His passionate prayer was repeated again and again, each time with more urgency "Lord, help me."

After several seconds a voice came from heaven, "What do you wish?"

"Save me," the man responded in panic.

After a few moments the voice from heaven responded, "Okay, let go of the branch."

After a brief pause the man shouted, "Is there anyone else up there?"

That is the way we are about change – we hold on to what we have and never see what adventures lay ahead. We do not want to change because we do not want to let go of the things we have. The truth is we are fearful of losing what we have, so we are never able to achieve our ultimate destiny.

When change is in the wind, each person wonders, "How will it impact me, will I lose my influence, will I gain influence."

Five things I know about change:

1. Change is inevitable

2. Change causes conflict

3. Change requires courage

4. There will always be those who oppose change

5. True change cannot be imposed from the outside.

Whether we like it or not change is inevitable. Things are going to change. Ancient philosopher Heraclitus of Ephesus, [50] was known for his doctrine of change. He wrote in the fifth century BCE,

> *"No man can put his foot in the same river twice, everything flows, nothing stands still, and ...Nothing endures but change."*

If the roots of the organization are strong, it can be returned to its earlier glory by reestablishing the things that have been lost or forgotten. The roots of the organization are found in its core values. If you want it to be renewed, you must go back and reestablish its original vision, values, priorities, and practices.

Changing Organizational Culture

Within any established organization there are unwritten rules and codes of conduct and a philosophy of life which are hard to change. Charles Duhigg, writes that these behavior habits may be deliberate or a result of historic issues.

---

[50] Greek philosopher, Heraclitus of Ephesus (c. 535 BC – 475 BC)

Building to Last

"There are no organizations without institutional habits. There are only places where they are deliberately designed, and places where they are created without forethought, so they often grow from rivalries or fear."[51]

Too often we have found leaders that attempt to transform their organizations by merely changing programs and styles. They see another group or competitor that is successful and think they can duplicate that success by implementing what they see others doing. Often these changes alienate the established customers while failing to attract the target groups. Merely changing programs is not often successful because of the underlying culture - personalities, philosophies, and habits of the organization.

When an organization knows who it is, what its strengths are, and what it is trying to accomplish, it can respond intelligently to changes from its environment. Whatever it decides to do is determined by this clear sense of self, not just because a new trend or market has appeared. The organization does not get locked into supporting certain products or business units just because they exist, or following after every fad just because it shows up. The presence of a clear identity makes the organization less vulnerable to its environment; it develops greater freedom to decide how it will respond.[52]

A clear sense of self begins with the core values of the organization and leads to the priorities. When these are lost, the organization will drift into institutionalization. The re-establishment

[51] Duhigg, Charles (2012-02-28). The Power of Habit: Why We Do What We Do in Life and Business (p. 160). Random House Publishing Group. Kindle Edition.
[52] Wheatley, Margaret J. (2006-09-01). Leadership and the New Science: Discovering Order in a Chaotic World (Kindle Locations 1399-1403). Berrett-Koehler Publishers. Kindle Edition.

and emphasis on values, priorities and vision can change the company.

On Monday morning a friend was driving me to the Seattle -Tacoma airport after a long weekend of teaching and leading. On the way he asked me a question which caused me to think, "What do you feel is the best thing about your new situation?"

I had not considered that and did not have a ready answer. My early years were spent as a corporate executive in the electronics industry, starting and growing business organizations. Leaving that behind, we transitioned into full time ministry - planting and growing churches and teaching and leading seminars and workshops. The new situation was semi-retirement. We had left our church, moved to Mississippi, and started Aslan Ministries - a non-profit organization to encourage and equip churches and other organizations.

A good answer to his question might have been, "less pressure," or "more independence," but after about thirty seconds of thought, realized the true significance of my situation, "Now I have time to think."

Throughout my multiple careers, I lived in a culture of busyness. Too often, the priorities of life include filling our lives with busy stuff. As long as we are moving or doing something, we are progressing. We get so caught up with daily activities that we never have the time to reflect. Our culture has become too organized.

How does culture change? Changing the culture of an organization requires a change in values, priorities and practices. The organizational DNA must be changed. It will take a powerful leader or a large enough group within the organization with a fresh vision to change or restore the value system. There are two factors which determine whether the organization is able to change its culture.

159

First, the size of the organization affects its ability to change. It is like a ship at sea. A ski boat can maneuver rapidly while an aircraft carrier requires miles to turn around. Small organizations are more maneuverable just because of the pure mass required to change.

The second factor is where the organization is in its life cycle. An organization in its "initial structuring" phase would be easier to change than one operating at "maximum efficiency," and an organization in the "Institutionalization" phase is extremely difficult to turn.

Cultural change will only happen by changing the core values resulting in changes to priorities and practices. Many organizations reject change even when it is the only hope of survival.

A new general manager was brought in to run a Louisiana organization. He was full of excitement and had a five year vision for the organization. The vision had six specific goals. It did not take long after arriving to realize that there were serious problems; morale was low, financially there was a negative cash flow, and there were no plans to turn the organization around. In fact he was not sure that they could even pay his salary. The organization was divided by two warring factions. In six months the organization was beginning to turn around and the new leader received his first full paycheck. But there was still a morale problem as the two factions had not come together.

At the end of three years the organization turned the corner and became a well-functioning organization.

How was the transformation accomplished? The single most important change was organizational which in turn helped change the culture. The morale problem had been fueled by a perception that each groups concerns were not heard nor considered when decisions were made. Rather than fighting things out in board meetings, regular informal

160

meetings were conducted where everyone was allowed share their concerns. After listening to all inputs, the leader still had the hard decisions to make, but everyone had input. This cooperative leadership approach not only transformed the morale of the organization, but it provided more creativity in decision making.

At one of the first meetings the issue that needed the most work was this area of morale. Meeting in groups of four or five, (Quality circles) each group discussed how they could improve morale. Each group presented their recommendations. Everyone agreed to accept the recommendations. No official action was taken, nor was it required. It was not imposed upon them by the leader. The members of the organization owned it themselves. As a result, a year later "Morale was the number one item that was working well. It had become a value and was reflected in the actions of the people.

In this example, the culture was able to change because it was relatively small and young. It had only existed for three years prior to the e change in leadership. Being small and young it was not too difficult to change the values, priorities and practices. The organization had been in the "formal organizing" stage and not reached "maximum efficiency." Large organizations with more traditions are harder to change.

Changing an organization culture is a complex issue. Organizations are built from the ground up. Corporate core values are those brought in by the founding leaders. Based upon their values, they establish certain priorities which result in specific practices. A new leader cannot just bring in new practice or program and expect things to change. Change must be a surgical operation to the values, the priorities, and priorities without killing the patient.

In government, we have many examples of the failure to transform a nation without first changing the values system. The mere acts of passing of legislation, regulating conduct, and initiating new practices, does not effectively combat prejudice and eliminate racialism. These are only transformed by first changing the system of values inherent in the population. Once core values change, priorities and practices begin to change resulting in a changed national culture.

Changing of values is most easily accomplished in young organizations and in the young people of an organization or nation. Values may also be changed by desperation - when continuing organizational systems become so difficult that people must change their values or die.

It may be a simple matter of modernizing the processes, changing the methods of communicating, or as Google found successful, take away everyone's office.

> *We strive to maintain the open culture often associated with startups, in which everyone is a hands-on contributor and feels comfortable sharing ideas and opinions. In our weekly all-hands ("TGIF") meetings — not to mention over email or in the cafe — Googlers ask questions directly to Larry, Sergey and other execs about any number of company issues. Our offices and cafes are designed to encourage interactions between Googlers within and across teams, and to spark conversation about work as well as play*[53]

Organizational Renewal

Renewal begins inside of an individual, then spreads to others, and eventually it will renew the organization. But it must start with someone. That person does not have to be the leader, nor have any high position. It requires a vision, a passion, and the courage to share with others.

When institutionalism sets in, the vision, purpose and/or mission of the organization is pushed away in favor of survival. The mission becomes one of keeping the organization

---

[53] http://www.google.com/about/company/facts/culture/

from dying. All the effort and resources are used to service the organization. Leaders have become managers of the assets rather than entrepreneurs. In a church, the leader now has become a chaplain rather than evangelist or spiritual leader. The focus is on survival. Change can come by (1) reigniting the vision that started the organization, (2) changing the form of doing business (Business Model), (3) reducing or eliminating structure, and (4) refocusing on the mission.

"Why would we change something that has been working so well?" That is the question that sports commentators asked super golfer Tiger Woods when after winning many major championships, he changed his golf swing and his coach. In fact at this writing he has done that four times. It is the same question asked of Padraig Harrington, the great Irish golfer who began to change his swing soon after winning three major championships in a little over a year. There answer was that there was something missing in what they were trying to do. And, as their bodies aged, the changes were necessary to keep up with the physical changes.

The purpose or mission of those golfers, to win tournaments, did not change, but their method of achieving victory changed to extend their careers and improve their capabilities.

Making changes is uncomfortable to many, but it is this that causes attitudes to change.

What is lost is the vision which fuels the fire. How do we regain that fire that once permeated the organization? The values may still be there, the priorities may still be in place, but the practices need to change.

Over a century ago the little country of Wales experienced a national revival that had an impact around the world. The revival brought in one hundred thousand new converts to faith. Within months the movement spread throughout the world. This move of God had very small beginnings. It did not always but began with teenagers. Florrie Evans while attending a youth group meeting in February of 1904 declared publicly that she loved the Lord Jesus with all her heart. With these words the Spirit seemed to fall on the meeting and the fire quickly spread to other young people in the Cardiganshire area. Later that year Evangelist Seth Joshua was addressing a Convention which included the young people five miles north of Cardigan. Seth himself had been praying for years that God would raise up a young man from the pits to revive the churches. On Thursday September 29th 1904 his prayer was answered as twenty six year old, student, Evan Roberts experienced a dramatic conversion.

Evan Roberts, his brother Dan, and his best friend Sidney began traveling the country holding revival meetings with a difference. This was a Revival with youth on fire. Young Florrie and her friend Maud went on a team to North Wales using their voices as instruments of God's message. A storm of love and power completely transformed lives. People's live were dramatically changed. The crime rate dropped, drunkards were reformed, pubs reported losses in trade. Bad language disappeared. It was reported that the pit ponies failed to understand their born again colliers who seemed to speak without curse and blasphemy. Even football and rugby became uninteresting in the light of new joy and direction received by the Converts.

In the renewal process, the changing of practices provides a momentum. When institutionalism sets in the original practices become traditions no longer supporting the priorities and purpose. They have a life of their own that must be maintained. We often hear the sigh, "We have always done it that way."

Removing traditions may be traumatic for many in the organization, but it is required if renewal is to be accomplished. This is where many organizations lose their opportunity for renewal. They simply do not want to disturb the status quo.

Organizations require regular pruning of the practices which are not bearing fruit.

Disorganize or Bust

While we have lusted for order in organizations, we have failed to understand where to find it. We have seen order reflected in the structures we build, whether they be bright mirror-glass buildings, dazzling charts, or plans begun on paper napkins. These structures take so much time, creativity, and attention that it is hard not to want them to be permanent.[54]

Structure is the enemy of creativity. Structure, while necessary can have the unwanted effect of reducing creativity. In this day and age, creative problem solving has become paramount in boardrooms around the world. Where large corporations previously sought out individuals with MBA degrees from prestigious schools, now they are seeking creative people with Masters Degrees in "Fine Arts."

In addition to suppressing creativity, structure tends to have a life of its own as Parkinson's Law clearly shows. The bureaucracy's main purpose is to expand and perpetuate its existence. Eliminating unfruitful elements of the structure will break the cycle of the ever expanding consumption of resources within the organization.

Pruning is a horticultural practice that involves the removal of branches, buds, and deadwood to improve or maintain the health of a tree, plant or flower. Pruning increases both the quantity and the quality of flowers and fruits. This practice targets diseased, damaged, dead, non-productive, or otherwise unwanted tissue from the crop.

---

[54] Wheatley, Margaret J. (2006-09-01). Leadership and the New Science: Discovering Order in a Chaotic World (Kindle Locations 559-562). Berrett-Koehler Publishers. Kindle Edition.

Organizations are living organisms that will benefit from regular pruning. Each practice, program and individual in the organization must be evaluated and those which are diseased, damaged, dead, non-productive, or otherwise unwanted must be removed. We cannot eliminate all structure, but must be merciless in trimming outdated structure and return to the concept of structure following function.

John 15:1-2 (NKJV) "I am the true vine, and My Father is the vine dresser. Every branch in Me that does not bear fruit He takes away; and every branch that bears fruit He prunes, that it may bear more fruit.

If you have enjoyed this book share it with a friend

Sshare a review on Amazon.com

Made in the USA
Middletown, DE
01 June 2019